T0083528

Karolinum Press

Jacques Rossi
Fragments of Lives
Chronicles of the Gulag

in collaboration with Sophie Benech

VÁCLAV HAVEL SERIES

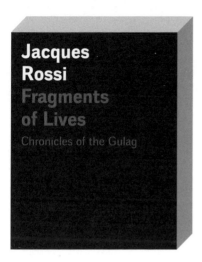

Jacques
Rossi
Fragments
of Lives
Chronicles of the Gulag

KAROLINUM PRESS

KAROLINUM PRESS
Karolinum Press is a publishing department of Charles University
Ovocný trh 560/5, 116 36 Prague 1, Czech Republic
www.karolinum.cz

Originally published in French under the title *Fragments de Vies*
by Cherche midi éditeur
http://www.jacques-rossi-goulag.org

Text © Jacques Rossi, 2018
Translation © Marie-Cécile Antonelli-Street, 2018
Illustrations © Jacques Rossi, 2018
Postface © Sophie Benech, 2018

Cover and graphic design by /3.dílna/
Frontispiece photo author's archive
Set and printed in the Czech Republic by Karolinum Press
First English edition

Cataloguing-in-Publication Data is available from the National Library
of the Czech Republic

ISBN 978-80-246- 3700-6
ISBN 978-80-246-3721-1 (pdf)
ISBN 978-80-246-4215-4 (epub)
ISBN 978-80-246-4214-7 (mobi)

CONTENTS

Fragments
of Lives

THE SPARROW, THE COW, AND THE CAT

"This isn't university, you know! You've gotta think!" exclaimed Ahmed Souleimanov. He had just finished telling me how to hold the handle of the pickaxe so that your wrists wouldn't hurt, and how to use this archaic tool so that you wouldn't damage your back.

It might well be that Ahmed didn't have a clue as to what a university was. Maybe he was only parroting a popular wisecrack often thrown out by the experienced veterans towards raw newcomers who just happened to have an intellectual look about them.

Ahmed, a forty-eight year old Eastern Siberian Tatar, had done his first stint in the Gulag at the age of sixteen for petty theft. Since then he had returned on a regular basis, sometimes for perfectly legitimate reasons, often because – as he already had a police record – they substituted him for a criminal they were incapable of catching. It was a common practice made easier by the fact that according to Soviet law, the investigation and examination are both done in the same office, which also happened to be the office responsible for drawing up charges. At any rate, Ahmed could boast a prodigious knowledge of the arcania of the Soviet Gulag and of Soviet life in general. I genuinely appreciated the teachings and theoretical remarks that he generously dispensed in my direction. To make these points easier to grasp, he frequently spoke in parables, such as the following:

One fine day in the middle of winter, the Siberian sun started shining (which sometimes happens). Encouraged by these rays full of promise, a sparrow left his hiding place and, feeling happy, started fluttering in the beautiful blue sky. However, sun or no sun, at -50°C, the little wings of this foolhardy bird just froze. He fell like a stone into the snow bank, dead. But, as luck would have it, a cow came along and dropped a pile of dung right on top of the little bird. This life-saving heat instantly revived our little bird and, elated, he poked his head out of the muck, and started to chirp. A cat happened to hear this, came close to him, pulled him delicately from the pile, cleaned him off carefully, and then ate him.

"The moral of the story," said Ahmed, "he who shits on your head doesn't necessarily mean you any harm, and he who pulls you out of shit doesn't necessarily mean you well – and when you find yourself in deep shit, it is perhaps nothing to chirp about!"

Thanks to my friend and professor, Ahmed, I learned a great truth: if in a given situation I see no logic, it is not that there is none, but that I am incapable of perceiving it.

A COMMONPLACE STORY

"Confess! Confess! You swine! Confess your anti-Soviet activities, you dirty fascist! You pile of shit!"

Since last night I have been standing up in the interrogator's office (1). I am in Moscow's notorious Lubyanka (2) Prison, and I'm not sure what is happening to me. Just a few weeks ago in Spain I was risking my life for Lenin's cause, and now here I am in Moscow accused of being a dirty fascist by a Soviet interrogator...

"Confess! Confess! You dirty fascist! Pile of Shit! You scumbag!" It's daytime and another tormentor has taken over.

"Confess! Confess! You dirty fascist!"

I've been here over twenty-four hours, standing with my hands behind my back. Is it the result of stress? I feel neither fatigue nor hunger. After forty-eight hours the interrogator summons a guard, signs a slip, and hands it to him. The guard takes me out. As we go by a desk, a sergeant takes the signed paper that my guard hands him, writes something in a big register book, and covers the page with a large metal jacket. A narrow slit in the sheet allows me to see only the line that concerns me, hiding the rest of the page.

"Sign here!" says the sergeant, giving me a pencil.

I see my name, the date and time. Five forty-three. It was the same procedure when I arrived two days ago. The guard makes me walk in front of him. He repeatedly strikes a key against his belt buckle. In some prisons this signal is replaced by a clicking of the tongue. At each turn, in the hallway, or doorway, he orders me: "Halt! Face the wall!" then he makes sure that no guard with another prisoner is coming the other way. This to prevent any fortuitous meetings between prisoners. Nothing is left to chance. In every one of the thousands of Soviet prisons no prisoner will ever encounter another, anywhere, unless it was so arranged or tolerated by the authorities. It has been like this for generations.

Finally here I am in front of my cell door.

"Halt!" The guard on duty approaches my escort, glances at the slip of paper handed to him, and opens the door. Throughout the entire trip I've kept my hands behind my back, as per the rules. Robot-like I cross the threshold the same way. All the faces in the cell turn towards me. What a pleasure to be "home" again, in one's own cell! I collapse onto the fifty centimetres of common berth that is allotted to me. Without asking any questions, one of my neighbours takes off my shoes and rubs my swollen legs. Someone brings me last night's soup. At each meal they've refilled it. I'm not hungry. I'm exhausted. I melt to sleep. Everything goes blank.

Suddenly, my name shouted out hits me like a bludgeon and the door flings open. As soon as it shuts behind me, isolating me from my cell companions, the guard asks me my name while simultaneously looking at his slip. I answer. His two henchmen twist my arms. They will only let me go to sign the sergeant's big register book, and lead me into the interrogator's office.

"Confess, you dirty fascist, confess!" "I have nothing to confess," I say from time to time. Each time this unleashes a new outburst of anger from the interrogator. They interrogate me in shifts of five to six hours each. I remain standing, hands behind my back for five days, and six nights in a row. By then I'm not really aware of what's going on around me. The Klieg light disappears. I'm walking... Then I'm being led down the hallways... Have I signed the sergeant's big book? ... The door opens... How good it feels to be back in my cell!

They come back and fetch me just a few moments later. This time it isn't the usual route. Where are they taking me? Never mind as long as it's not to the interrogator's office! They lead me down the basement, past some cellars, through a door. A barren windowless room with a plain light bulb shining down on a concrete slab floor. There are several dark and damp blotches, a faucet, and a full pail of water. A corporal and two soldiers are standing with their backs against the wall. They wipe sweat from their forehead. The corporal glances at the slip of paper that my guard hands him. He sticks it onto a protruding nail with quite a few others on it already. Without a word they start to beat me. I don't know how I end up on the concrete floor. Blur... I open my eyes. I look up and see one of the men with an empty pail in his hand. I realize that I've just been splashed. They stand me back up and start to beat me again. They punch me and kick me with their boots. Before I faint again I see the insignia of the Communist Youth League on the corporal's lapel: the profile of Lenin on a red banner. The same Lenin for whom I risked my life in Spain.

Fifty years have gone by. I have seen much worse since. Yet, those three young men are clearly etched in my memory. What kind of methods did the authorities use to mutilate their souls and thus turn them into monsters? After all, I was probably the one who fared better... They were the first to torture me in the name of what I believed to be the promise of brighter days to come.

NOTES
(1) Russian dictionaries translate the word *sledovatel* into "prosecutor" which was accurate in the Tsar period and during the few months following the 1917 February Revolution. As of the Bolshevik coup d'état, the preliminary investigation, the arrest, the instruction and sentence are handled by a single institution, i.e. the state police. The word "prosecutor" being misleading for any Western reader, we opted for "commissar-interrogator."
Most of the time, the trial was meant to condemn the convict to a pre-determined sentence. One of my co-inmates, arrested by the Nazis then freed by the Soviets who then arrested him again, told me, "The Gestapo would torture me so that I would tell the truth, the KGB so that I would lie."

(2) In December 1918, the Tcheka relocated its headquarters in what used to be the property of the pre-revolutionary *Rossiia* insurance

company, on Lubianka Square, renamed Dzerzhinskii in 1926. Inside this seven-story building is the most "Hilton-like" of all Soviet pre-trial prisons. It housed many VIPs and lots of foreigners. Executions took place there too.

A LESSON ON DIALECTICS

Aristocratic look. Aquiline nose. Sturdy. Solid. White, well-fed complexion. Piercing stare. Handsome. Two weeks ago Boris Matveievitch was still a business representative for the U.S.S.R. in Mexico. For the last twelve days he's been my neighbour on the lower bunk in the Butyrka Prison (1) of Moscow. His interrogator was after him right away, harassing him. Every morning, at about five o'clock, they would bring him back into his cell after an all-night session.

Much later I learned that the night interrogators earned large bonuses. As for the prisoner once brought back in his cell, he is not allowed to close his eyes until lights out, and every evening they would come and fetch Boris Matveievitch for another all-night session. During the day in his cell he wouldn't utter a single word. His eyes saw no one. In his stare you could read his dismay. He hardly touched the bread that was distributed in the morning, the gruel at noon, nor the soup at night. He was wasting away. The interrogations were turning him into a rag doll.

One day in the showers I was surprised to see him come out of his shell: he very conscientiously washed his brown and white checked foreign-made handkerchief. But once in his cell Boris Matveievitch fell back into his usual apathy. Robotically he would hold his handkerchief in his hand to let it dry.

Occasionally, on his way back from the showers, someone would realize they had been missing their towel or handkerchief, and then a voice would cry out, "Has anyone seen my green and white handkerchief?" Boris Matveievitch, looking a bit haggard, would then break out of his silence. "I'm sorry, here it is," he would say humbly. The man would have a closer look, "No, this isn't mine." And resume his search: "Has anyone seen a green and white handkerchief?" All along Boris Matveievitch firmly believed that the handkerchief that he had just washed and held in his hand was the one that the other man was looking for.

Several of us tried to convince him that the one in his hand was actually his own. In vain...

NOTES

(1) Butyrka: the former barracks for Her Majesty Catherine the Great's Butyrki Hussar Regiment was converted into one of the largest prisons in the late 19th century in Moscow. It was designed to house more than 3,000 prisoners but exceeded the number by far. During the Great Purge (1937), it housed about 20,000 prisoners, an approximate figure calculated by deduction. When I visited it in 1993, there were 6,000 prisoners.

TEARS AND LAUGHTERS

It's very early. The wake up call hasn't sounded yet. All of a sudden, silently, the door opens. Two guards come in dragging a lifeless body. They lay him down gently on the ground. We hear the head hitting the floor. Then the guards leave as they came without a word. The door closes. The man doesn't move. I go over to him. If it wasn't for his green sweater, I wouldn't have recognized him. He has a black eye, swollen lips, and his face is all bruised and covered with blood.

Rudi was away from his cell for five days and six nights. This uninterrupted interrogation must have been a painful ordeal. I place a wet rag over his burning forehead. Slowly he regains consciousness.

Several days go by. He is not summoned. Neither am I. A respite. For hours as to avoid Rudi's sinking into a deep depression, I tell him about books I have read, towns I have visited. He doesn't react. Finally I tell him about a rather special "cruise": the Comintern (1) had given me the assignment of carrying some secret documents from Genoa to an eastern Mediterranean port. For this affair they had supplied me with a false Swedish passport. I was looking forward to several days of rest and relaxation aboard the ship... No sooner had I embarked than the steward was all excited to let me know that there was another Swede among the passengers. I was going to have some company. I was immediately panic-stricken. If we bumped into each other he would guess in no time what type of a Swede I was... So I pretended I was sick, and throughout the entire trip I stayed closed up in my cabin.

At this Rudi suddenly smiled, and said, "The other *Swede* was me."

NOTES
(1) "The International Communist Party" founded in 1919 under the initiative of Lenin included all the Marxist-Leninist parties of the world. It was dissolved in 1943.

A DEBT OF GRATITUDE

In the good town of Saransk everyone knew the surgeon Vladimir Radionov, director of the largest regional hospital. He was loved for his skill, his devotion, and his generosity, not only amongst his own people, the Mordovians, who were justifiably proud of the success of one of their own, but also by the Russians who were busy imposing their Russian influence on this small ethnic minority by squashing their distinctive Finno-Ugric culture. He was indeed one of the most important people of Mordovia, and yet not a member of the nomenklatura.

One night the telephone rang. He heard a person's voice obviously upset on the other end. It was the barely recognizable voice of the NKVD (1) chief, General Petrov. His eight-year-old daughter Tania was suffocating. She was dying. The general had just sent his staff car to get the doctor. There was just time for him to dress and get his medical bag. He finds Tania in an alarming state. No time to waste. He makes an incision in her trachea, inserts a tube, and puts his lips on the tube to suck out the pus. The child immediately resumes breathing again. The general and his wife don't know how to thank the doctor.

Two years later, it's the time of the Great Purge (2). According to some logic that only very few victims seem able to grasp, Doctor Radionov has to go. His great renown makes him seen as a particularly despicable *enemy of the people* for which the punishment should be a bullet in the back of the neck. One can only imagine all the torture that he must have withstood to get him to sign the necessary confessions… Those confessions would be published in the newspapers, so that the indignant people would demand his death.

But events took an unexpected turn. As there had to be a big trial, General Petrov who had vowed his great and heartfelt thanks to the doctor, managed to get another equally innocent victim to fulfill the role of the despised *'enemy of the people.'* This did not mean, however, that Doctor Radionov was completely innocent, for that would entail the execution of the general as well as the doctor. Petrov thus decided to set up a common charge of 'anti-Soviet propaganda' that would impose the maximum of a ten-year sentence.

A few years later when I met the doctor at the Norilsk (3) camp, he showed a strong and genuine feeling of gratitude towards the general for having spared his life by arranging for such an insignificant ten-year sentence.

As he was an excellent doctor, he was quickly assigned to the health services of the camp, where he not only was charged with patching together the broken limbs of his fellow inmates but also caring for the administrative personnel. Even the director of the camp, General Panioukov, called on his considerable talents. Having just taken a very young bride, the General had some problems, and made Dr. Radionov his personal physician.

Thanks to the efforts of this general, completely legal and official strings were pulled to free Radionov two years early before his sentence. This in stark contrast to most other prisoners who at the end of their sentence were often detained under the infamous saying, *to be detained until further notice.* To express his gratitude, the doctor cared diligently for General Panioukov's health until the day he died.

As for the other General Petrov, he was unable to escape a bullet in the neck. After each successive wave of mass repression, there would follow a blood letting of a certain number of those responsible for the previous one. The good people of Russia called this *'the liquidation of the liquidators,'* and each time the criteria used to determine the victims were incomprehensible.

NOTES
(1) *Narodny Kommissariat Vnoutrennikh Del*:
"People's Commissariat of Internal Affairs." The USSR NKVD was formed on 10 July 1934, independent of the "Union Republic"

and the other Soviet republics already existing since the beginning. The OGPU (the USSR's United Main Political Administration which had replaced the GPU, State Political Administration, when the USSR was formed on 30 December 1922) then came under the jurisdiction of its State Security Department. Initiated on 20 December 1917 by Lenin, the GPU had replaced the Tcheka ("All Russian Extraordinary Commission Combating Counter-Revolution and Profiteering"). In 1941 the NKVD State Security Department of the USSR became the NKGB, the People's Commissariat of State Security. It underwent several changes, which I will spare the reader, and then disappeared for good after Stalin's death in 1953. Its functions were transferred to the USSR MVD—Ministry of Justice) since all the People's Commissariats were redesignated ministries on 15 March 1946. The NKVD thus became the MVD and on 13 March 1954 the infamous KGB (Committee for State Security) appeared.

(2) Purge: *tchistka*, literally "cleaning" or "washing". It refers to the gigantic wave of mass arrests followed by sentences of one or several categories of citizens. These purges would come systematically following Lenin and his Party's rise to power. The most famous in the Western world was that of 1936-38, known as the Great Purge, or that of "the year 1937," or just the "37th." It engulfed several million individuals from all walks of life, especially members of the Communist Party, considered "not to be devoted enough to Stalin." That's one of the problems I ran into. Torture was used to obtain the wanted "confessions." More than a million and a half people were shot. This Great Purge was essential for the Communist Party and its leader to establish absolute power. The Second Purge was between the years 1947-49. It isn't as well-known by foreigners, as is the case with the massacre of millions of peasants from 1929 to 1932 accompanying forced collectivization.

(3) Situated on the right bank of the Yenisei River, above the Arctic Circle. Temperatures drop to 50°C below in the winter. The ground thaws in the summer as far as forty centimeters deep. The first convoys of convicts arrived in the hold of barges in 1936 to extract nickel, copper, cobalt, and coal. They built the facilities and the factories of the future polymetallurgy complex, as well as the town, designed by engineers who were also prisoners. In 1956, the administrative center of the Gulag in charge of the non-iron metal work was redesignated into a ministry which was then the sole employer of the manual labor found in the forced labor camp of Norilsk.

JUST A MINUTE, PLEASE!

Fleeing the Nazis, a young Viennese cardiologist found refuge in Moscow. Siegfried and his wife Esther had never been Communists, but they admired Stalin's "humanism" for having generously offered refuge to the persecuted Jews. So here is Siegfried assigned to one of the biggest hospitals in Moscow. A young German-speaking student served as his interpreter for patients. Siegfried was able to withstand the surprising deprivations that confronted him at every turn, as much in the hospital, as in his daily life. However, what weighed most heavily on him was the all-pervasive oppression. He and Esther felt themselves strangled by invisible tentacles. Besides this, they found themselves butting up against a more or less budding anti-Semitism. All things considered, Esther remembered that she had an uncle who was a lawyer in New York. So why not try to immigrate to the United States? Uncle Isaac would surely help them, and the child that she was carrying would be American.

To their amazement the necessary paperwork required by the Soviet administration was complicated and difficult to fulfill. Before filling out their exit visa application, they were required to obtain notarized documents from countless offices they weren't even aware existed. A few of their Soviet friends, after assuring themselves that they were far from any indiscreet ears would tell them to give it up. "But why?" these naive people would wonder, the same people who had succeeded in escaping from Hitler. "To avoid the worst," murmured a friend with an enigmatic look on his face who knew what he was talking about.

Finally, after much dogged persistence, and thanks to the Vice-Minister of the Ministry of Health who intervened in person – something Siegfried might regret later on – there they were: Siegfried, Esther, and the newly arrived Rebecca, sitting in a first-class train compartment on the way to Riga, Lithuania. This is 1937, the Baltic Republics won't be invaded by the Soviet Union for another two years. In Riga, the family will embark on a steamer bound for New York. Their passage is reserved, and they are most excited and happy. One thing surprises them: none of their Moscow friends came to the train station to see them off.

The train starts moving. Tomorrow they will cross the border. They will leave Russia. They will reach Lithuania, Riga, then the boat for New York. Oh boy! How slow this train moves! The border is still far away in the distance when suddenly the train slows down. The Soviet border guards jump on while the train is still moving. There are many of them, each wearing a bright Chartreuse cap. In every coach the first compartment is reserved for them, and that's where they set up their headquarters. A Soviet train conductor guards the other end of the car. Without a word they check the hallway looking into each compartment with a piercing glare. If the curtains are drawn, they go in to open them, still without a word. It is only after this preliminary inspection that the actual procedure begins: all the passengers are expected to remain in their compartment. One of the officers asks each person for his passport. He opens it, looks at the photo, then with utmost purpose scrutinizes the face of the bearer and looks again at the photo. Once satisfied with his examination, he closes the passport and hands it to his colleague. With a blank expression the latter accepts it and puts it in his left hand on top of the others. Then begins the nit-picking inspection of the luggage. Before they begin with the suitcases and the packages, they look under the seats, they lift up the cushions, etc.

At last they reach the border. The train stops between two rows of armed guards. The train station is very small. There's much coming and going amongst border guards loaded with official papers. Two or three civilians are leaning up against a wall, staring out into space. A railroad workman, covered in axel grease, walks besides the train and raps each axle rod with a long-handled hammer. A border guard accompanies a passenger over to the mailbox, and motions to him to slip his letter into the mailbox. The passenger explains in German that he saw no harm in agreeing to deliver a letter from a friend in Moscow to another friend in Riga, where he was going anyway. "The postal services here are more reliable," the guard assures him. The envelope then slides down into the "reliable" Soviet mailbox. The passenger is escorted back to his compartment. Whew! Time goes by. Two guards appear for a last look at the photos and then return the passports to Siegfried. What a relief! He carefully places the precious passports into the inside pocket of his suit, right next to the Moscow-Riga and Riga-New York tickets. Will the train ever leave?

One of the guards returns. He steps up into the wagon. A deathly silence fills the coach. You can hear his steps in the hallway. He stops in front of their compartment. "Just a minute, please!," he says to Siegfried with a lighthearted air. "Please follow me!" "Don't worry," he adds with a benevolent smile, "It's a mere formality, the train won't leave without you."

When I met Siegfried at the Butyrka Prison in Moscow in 1938, he had already been there for eight months. He had not heard anything about Esther, and their little girl. The NKVD accused him of spying for Nazi Germany. After a while I was transferred elsewhere, and I never saw him again. However, ten years later while I was in the immense transit prison in Krasnoyarsk I met a certain Volodia. This is what he told me: After his military service, and so as not to return to the *kolkhoz* and its brutal and mind numbing work, Siegfried was hired as a camp guard in Norilsk. There he met Maroussia, one of the prison nurses. One of the inmates, a stretcher-bearer, had told her Siegfried's sad story: for ten years he had no news from his wife and daughter. He begged Maroussia to mail a letter to his wife's family in New York for he had no access to any correspondence. At first she refused. To get her job she had signed an agreement stating that she would comply with the rules regarding relations with the inmates. Any infraction would be prosecuted. She, however, also had a soft heart, and was herself expecting a baby.

Of course she wouldn't mail the letter to New York from Norilsk. That would have alerted the local NKVD. Instead, she sent it to a very dear childhood friend, Tania, who lived in Moscow. A letter to the United States sent from Moscow would arouse fewer questions. Tania couldn't refuse such a favor. They had grown up together, and when her mother had been arrested Maroussia's family had taken her in.

How did the NKVD manage to find out about the letter? In any case, Tania was brought to the authorities. They explained the seriousness of her action. What action? Of not having reported Maroussia. However, all would be forgotten if Tania would seduce a certain foreign diplomat, and if she would allow herself to be photographed in compromising poses with the man. She was disgusted and incensed about the whole thing, but understood the danger.

"Comrade," she said in an effort to stall, "to get my job as a guide I made a commitment not to cross certain lines in my relations with foreigners, at the risk of legal action..." "Don't worry about that. Those lines are the ones **we** set up..." The comrade solemnly promised Tania that if she cooperated she would have no trouble at work, and her friend Maroussia as well would be spared.

That done, she worried no more. She had successfully passed the first test, and the NKVD kept her on hand for other "patriotic feats." As for Maroussia – who was no longer of use to them – she was condemned to ten years of hard labor for "high treason." Her husband, Volodia, got away with only five, for "failure to be vigilant and failure to denounce a crime against the security of the state."

The poor stretcher-bearer was none other than Siegfried, the Viennese cardiologist. He had known how to escape the Nazis, but not the Soviets.

A NEVER-ENDING STORY

They had just brought him into our cell. His name was Lekhowitch. He had been an engineer in a factory at Lioubertsy, near Moscow. He had been arrested by the local police who then handed him over to the care of the NKVD. There he fell into the hands of an interrogator of unequalled cruelty, or so he thought. He who had fled Poland under Pilsudski to seek refuge in the land of socialism had never seen such a monster before. He just couldn't get over it: the non stop interrogations for days, going on night after night without respite, standing up, with new interrogators every three hours.

"What d'ya want, it's assembly line work," commented someone laconically.

For us there was nothing new in that. Lekhowitch pressed on: "One fine day, it all stopped. I had been left in my cell for a whole week without being summoned. A real vacation! Then one night they came to get me. They led me to the interrogator's office where behind the table there was an unfamiliar face. The new interrogator told me that his former colleague had just been unmasked. He was one of Hitler's agents. "Then I'll be freed!" I said to myself. Quite the contrary: "Tell us what the two of you have been scheming, you piece of shit!" The new interrogator proved himself to be even more cruel than his predecessor. Thank God I was transferred here. I can still hear his falsetto. He was a redhead with a twitch in his left eye and a row of steel teeth across the front."

"Didn't he have a scar on his chin?" asked a great beanpole, who had only been brought into our cell two hours ago.

"Yes!" answered Lekhowitch. "You had to deal with him too?"

"In a way," he responded. "It is I who arrested him yesterday."

Who knows... Perhaps in a few minutes we'll see the one who arrested the beanpole this morning walk right in here. It's a never-ending story...

PENKHOS KARLIK

Three streams of urine noisily fall into the toilet bucket. Two of them are maize yellow, the third—Penkhos Karlik's—is red. He has just undergone a rough interrogation lasting several days straight. The bruises on his face are going from black to yellow passing through every shade of blue on their way. His back, especially his kidney area, is covered with half-moon shaped contusions from the boot heels that the interrogators laid into him. The entire barrack got to admire them recently in the showers.

In this particular cell of Moscow's Butyrka Prison in 1937, there are ninety-six inmates.

While squinting at me with one eye because the other is just an impressive swollen-shut shiner, he makes the following observation: "For Jacques, it's easier, it's not his country!"

I think I understand him. Karlik realizes that this unlivable hell-pit of which we are witnesses and victims is going to engulf generations of martyrs from all nationalities subjugated to the tyranny of Russian bolshevism. For Jacques, the Frenchman, this hell affects only him personally, not his entire nation, not his homeland, not his history, not his culture. I admit that this is in fact a consolation in some way.

Penkhos Karlik, a captain in the Red Army and commanding officer of an armored squadron, has been captured, as have many others, in the cogs of the Great Purge. He was accused of sabotaging his own machines. He was a sincere patriot, a loyal soldier, and couldn't understand how he could be expected to admit 'the facts' that were totally fabricated. Nevertheless, after six months of torture and total isolation, alone against his persecutors he gave up. He was scared that he would go insane. He admitted to 'the facts.' The torture immediately stopped, and he was back in his peaceful cell. *La dolce vita!*

However, eight days later, here he was brought back before his interrogator who, as if nothing was wrong, asks him to give his first name and patronym, date and place of birth, before suddenly scream-ing: "Son of a bitch! Who ordered you to sabotage the machines?"

The interrogator insists that Karlik turn in his general, a man Karlik admires and respects. He'd rather be tortured to death than cause him any problems.

I never saw Karlik again. However in 1953, fifteen years later, and some six thousand kilometers further east, I found myself sharing a cell with a former general. "It is largely because of my officers that I was only given a twenty-five year sentence," he said to me. "Not a single one would have given up under torture. Almost every other general has been shot." He could hardly believe his luck at having gotten such a light sentence. And yet, he could bearly walk: both legs had been broken during his torture, and had not been properly set at the prison hospital. It was Karlik's general. Isaac Borissovitch, attorney general before his arrest and sentence in 1937, confided in me later that if the general had been spared it was because he hadn't received any clear orders from the party.

THE COOLER

Three steps long, three steps wide. A cement floor weeping with moisture. No window, just a naked light bulb shining above the door day and night. A metal grate protects it. The only furniture in the room is the latrine bucket. It is dank and putrid. Before the administration built these cells they dug a big ditch and filled it with water. In the fall it turned into a slab of ice. Here in the Arctic it won't budge. It will also be the foundation for the solitary confinement, and will forever guarantee that whatever is built on top of it will be freezing. This is the "cooler" in which I must spend the next fifteen days and nights.

Besides this type of solitary confinement, there are other special ones in pretrial prisons. Under the orders of the interrogator, the inmates from whom they wish to extract certain confessions are thrown into these: the "sweat-box" that has a special pipe leading into it spitting out scalding steam; the "cold cooler"; or the "water "— flooded with water so that the inmate has his feet constantly in cold water up to his ankles or sometimes even up to his knees. Another variant is the inclined-floor cooler where the inmate ends up with his feet bent at an excruciatingly painful angle. Not to mention the one I call "Procustus' cooler" which is so narrow, and the ceiling so low it forces the prisoner to remain bent over.

Here in the cooler I'm free to take three steps in back and forth, or stand in the middle of the cell. If I lean against the walls, or squat on the floor I get instantly wet. The daily routine begins at 5 am, and ends at 11 pm. Staggering from sleep deprivation, I listen to the doors opening and closing. They're coming closer. At last it's my turn. The door opens, and the guard lets me pick up my clothing that has been left in the hallway in front of the door. During the day only underwear is permitted. Then he shows me my "bed." It is made of three long boards about six feet long, held together by two cross braces about twenty eight inches wide. I put my "bed" right on the floor, quickly throw on my clothes, fall onto my planks and go to sleep instantly.

Have I been asleep long? It's the frigid cold that wakes me up. I am shivering. I can't take it any longer. I get up to try to warm myself by pacing back and forth. Behind the little door hatch the guard orders me to lie back down. It is forbidden to get up before five o'clock, else you get another punishment. I comply and lie back down, and go back to sleep. Once again the cold wakes me up. It gets into my bones. I get up again to get warm. There's no reaction from the guard. I wonder if he's sleeping? I go back to sleep. And so forth, and so on about twenty times. Finally the factory siren blows. What a joy! This horrible night is over.

"Go back to bed!" orders the guard. It was the midnight siren and not the morning siren so that I have only got one hour of night behind, and still four more to go.

Before getting locked into one of the solitary confinement cells, the prisoner is thoroughly searched. He is stripped down to his underwear. He will get his clothing back each night before bedtime. Cigarettes, tobacco, matches, the smallest scraps of paper, any stubs of pencils or lead, any reading material, all of this is confiscated. Each morning he can have a cup of hot water, and three hundred grams of rye bread, and every day at noon a ladle full of very clear soup.

There is yet another problem: the inmate must learn how to arrange his body on the planks as to minimize suffering. If you lie on your back almost all the bones are in direct contact with the wood, from the occipital skull bone all the way down to the heels: the shoulder blades, the vertebrae, the sacrum, etc. Furthermore, if the head lies directly on the planks, your neck will be stiff by morning. Flipped over on the stomach is no more comfortable. But if you lie on your right side, and bring the left knee up to your chest you can counterbalance the weight of the left hip and relieve the right side of the torso. You put your right arm along your right side, and you put your right eye socket as well as the right cheekbone on the out-stretched fingers of your left hand which becomes the pillow. From time to time you may switch sides. Unfortunately, there is nothing that can be done about the cold.

After fifteen days, my punishment is over and I'm taken back to my regular cell. I can't wait to get out of my cold, clammy clothes. When I unbutton my jacket a moldy smell wafts up to my nose. Boy, it feels so good to be back in my cell!

Most often you are sentenced to solitary confinement for periods of ten to fifteen days during which you don't ever get out, not even once. No walks, no baths. Normally you can be sent there for just breaking the rules, but you can be sent there for a wide variety of other fabricated reasons too.

THE LETTER

This is 1937. We are in the Butyrka Prison in Moscow. There are more than sixty inmates in the cell. We can hear a timid rumbling, barely audible, that never gets louder for fear of violating the rule. It is forbidden to break the "silence of the penitentiary."

There is a slight shuffling behind the door. Everyone perks up his ears. The door doesn't open, but the little hatch does. We can see the guard's face behind it, just his eyes, his chin, and part of his hat's visor. His head is bent over. The cell door hatch is about four and one-half feet above the floor, which explains his position. Sixty pairs of eyes are now riveted on his lips.

"The letter M," he whispers.

We can hardly hear him. One of the younger ones who stood near the cell door hatch turns around and repeats what has been said. He too speaks most quietly.

Everyone whose last name does not begin with M breathes a sigh of relief. The 'M's they are looking for will certainly be interrogated.

"Mikhailov! answers an old engineer.

"Are there any others?"

"Mandelbaum."

"Who else?"

"Matveiv," answers a new one in a strangled voice. He's pale, and is shaking.

"First name and patronym."

"Ivan Borissovitch."

"Get ready according to the season!"

Matveiev looks feverishly for his jacket. One of his neighbors holds it out to him. It was right under his nose but he didn't see it. He puts it on, and in a deathly silence walks toward the door, which opens for him, and disappears.

This complex ritual, the strange formula with "The letter…," and whispering is in no way random. If the administration follows this sort of procedure it is for a specific reason: the guard might go to the wrong cell, and by calling someone's name who is not in that cell provides information to those in that cell of inmates who are in the other cells, and that they don't need to know about. In certain cases this information could be used to bolster a defense. As far as whispering, it is for the same reason: their co-detainees in other cells shouldn't know who is in the one next to them. It is important to note that following the ritual "First name and patronym?" The guard continues with further questions such as, "Article, sentence, end of term?"

The answers to these questions allow the guard to judge the level of danger presented by a particular prisoner. An inmate who is in for involuntary manslaughter is more dangerous than one in for a simple burglary, but less so than one who is in for premeditated murder. The most dangerous of all is of course the "political" prisoner. A man whose sentence only has a few months left is considered less dangerous than someone who has years left on his sentence.

As soon as the door is closed behind them, the "stroller" again asks the same questions over again. He checks his personal data with those written on the form in his hand. Everything corresponds. Two other guards twist the prisoner's arms. Their senior warder positions himself behind the group and orders: "Follow forward!" The prisoner, more dead than alive, moves forward between the two guards who don't let go even for an instant. He never bothers to ask where they are taking him. He knows that this ritual is reserved for those who will be interrogated.

NIKIFOR PROZOROV

1937: the Great Purge is at its peak. There are more than one hundred of us in a common cell at the Butyrka Prison in Moscow. There are Communist Party and Soviet bureaucrats, military men, engineers, students, diplomats, a stamp collector, two Esperanto speakers, a deaf-mute, several foreign Communists, and an old Bolshevik who joined the revolutions of 1905 and 1917. No one knows what's happening to them. We are all horror-stricken.

The door of the cell opens, and someone is pushed in. The door closes right behind him. The newcomer stands there, motionless, crushed by the enormity of his despair. Someone takes pity on him, talks to him, and asks him where he comes from. No response. Then he finally tells his story: his name is Nikifor Prozorov, he's 30 years old, and he is a farmer on a *kolkhoz*, near Moscow. One day, an old friend of his who had settled in Moscow showed him the *Moscow-Evening* newspaper. The newspaper carried an advertisement reading "Carpenter wanted! Inquire at Herzen St., Moscow, number so and so …" (I've forgotten which). He immediately thought that this could be an opportunity for him to escape the collective farm and the misery that it didn't hold any future. Thanks to his hard work on the farm, Prozorov managed to get a travel authorization from the director for a three-day visit to Moscow. He went to Herzen Street but couldn't find the right number, so he asked a policeman for directions. He was told that it was quite far, and difficult to find because of construction work but the policeman offered to drive him there. "People in Moscow sure are pleasant," he said to himself, touched, "unlike at home on the *kolkhoz*!" While this was happening, the policeman opened a small almost invisible box embedded in the side of a building which contained a telephone. He picked up the receiver, said a few words, and hung up. Almost at the same moment as he locked the box, a car pulled up and stopped right beside them. The policeman opened the door, and very kindly asked Prozorov to get in. "Wow, the folks in the capital sure are nice," he kept thinking, deeply moved by the kindness of the Moscovites. The ride in the car was fairly long... ending in prison.

All this happened only the day before. One of the inmates in the cell asks him, "Hey, was it number 'z' on Herzen St.?" "Yes, you're right!"answers Prozorov. "Ah, my poor fellow. That means you're a Japanese spy." Prozorov appears confused and doesn't understand anything. "It's not your fault, but you see, that's the address of the hotel where the Japanese Embassy staff stay. They have been looking for a carpenter for months. I have seen their letters to the Service Department of the Bureau of Foreign Affairs. They are the ones who handle all the problems of the foreign diplomats in Moscow. This is one way of preventing any contact between the local residents and the diplomatic personnel, and that's where I worked until I was arrested. It appears that the Japanese lost patience and placed an ad themselves."

During his first interrogation, the immediate question the interrogator would ask Prozorov is if he knows why he has been arrested. No, he has no idea. The interrogator helps him out by saying that it is for espionage, adding that the newspaper ad was a means for Japanese spies to contact their secret agents. "But I'm no Japanese secret agent!" protests Prozorov. "Prove it!" "Well, I've lived my entire life in the same village. At the age of seven I joined the Little Octobrists, at fourteen the Communist Youth League, and was admitted into the Communist Party during my military service. I'm not a Japanese spy!"

The sincerity and simplicity of this poor fellow won him the sympathy of the entire cell to such an extent that a committee was formed to request an appeal before the prosecution.

Weeks and months go by. Every time they bring Prozorov back from an interrogation he is more and more messed up. He wouldn't confess anything. Then the interrogations ended. Three months have gone by and now they finally take Prozorov away with "his belongings," signifying that he will be transferred to a new location, but where to? "They'll surely set him free," remarks one of the inmates who helped him draw up his many requests. One of them had him memorize his wife's phone number. "You tell her to send me forty five rubles next month, not fifty rubles as she usually does. That way I'll know that you've seen her. You tell her..." And everyone came to shake the lucky man's hand.

Two years later in 1939, I find myself in a convoy of prisoners sent towards an unknown destination – the inmates must never know what is awaiting them. They make us get off the train at Sverdlosk, or more precisely about one kilometer from Sverdlosk to avoid as much as possible any contact with the local population. We are brought under heavy guard on the way to the transit prison.

Once the registration procedures are completed, they separate us into several groups. My group is locked into a large common cell. It's packed. There are more than two hundred prisoners. Inmates are lying everywhere on the berths, tables, or floors. It is apparent that these people have many years of camp life behind them. I have never seen anything like it. A true vision of hell.

Then suddenly I hear my name, "Jacques!" In this crowd it is hard to determine just where that voice is coming from. Who would know me here when this is my first trip to Sverdlovsk. From underneath a berth, I see a large bearded man emerge with a wide smile. It's Prozorov. We greet each other like long lost brothers. He tells me he was sentenced to eight years in a forced labor camp charged with spying for Japan.

A COINCIDENCE

Once every ten days the inmates have the right to put their requests and complaints down on paper. They can direct them to any state, judicial or party authorities. So every ten days the senior warder asks us the same old question: "Does anyone want to fill out a request sheet?" In silence, the interested parties raise their hands, the senior warder counts them, marks the number in his notebook, and without a word closes the cell door hatch. A bit later it opens again. "Here are the writing materials," says the jailer in the usual regulation undertone.

He hands us an inkwell full of the inevitable purple ink, several fountain pens, and the exact number of sheets requested, or more precisely "a quarter of a sheet." On these postcard-sized pieces of paper some of the inmates pour out their grief in tiny handwriting, thirty or forty lines on each side. Just about all of them describe the absurd nature of the charges leveled against them, and condemn the methods used to extract confessions.

Contrary to what one would normally imagine, these heartfelt pleas for their souls and bodies did not end up in the trash. Ten years later several of us were astonished to find out that extracts of these complaints had been used to fabricate new accusations to extend sentences soon to be finished.

As soon as the guard sees through the hatch that we have all finished, he retrieves the inkwell and the fountain pens. As for the pieces of paper, it's not his duty. It's the local duty officer who comes and picks them up the following day. He comes in. Everyone is standing. Total silence reigns. This time it's an officer we've never seen before. He looks stern. Without saying a word he collects all the papers. Suddenly he recognizes one of the inmates and, apparently aggravated, asks: "Y-y-y-y-your n-n-n-n-ame?" The poor man, now livid, obeys: "P-p-p-p-petrachch-ch-ch-enkov." The local duty officer – now beet red – screams to the senior warder. "T-t-t-t-ten days in th-th-the c-c-c-c-c-cooler!"

The senior warder knows perfectly well that Petrachenkov stutters, but he remains impassive, and says nothing to contradict his superior. We all are biting our tongues to keep from bursting out in laughter. Ten days later Petrachenkov returned from the cooler much thinner than when he entered.

THE EXECUTIONER

K.D. is of Baltic origin, a former officer of the army of the tsar, member of an underground Bolshevik cell well before 1917, who later joined the first unit of Tcheka. A few years later he was appointed to Lenin's bodyguards.

We are in 1937 in Butyrka Prison. K. D. is my berth neighbor. When I say "neighbor," it's a figure of speech. There are well over five dozen of us lying, crammed against one another on the wood of what looks like a bridge of planks nailed to the wall of the cell. K.D. is a good neighbor, i.e. he won't trespass into my territory. He means well. Whenever I am subjected to some 'chain' interrogation, day and night with no interruption, he is the one who saves my bowl of soup. Sometimes he would reminisce about Lenin. He talks about him with much affection and admiration. I am surprised to see another side of Lenin, quite different than the one conveyed by the official propaganda. He is no longer a Bolshevik icon glued to his veneer, but rather a god of Olympus with many faults and shortcomings. K.D.'s message is also unconventional: he doesn't use any clichés, always refers to "the October coup" whereas for many years it has been renamed "The Great October Revolution of the Proletariat."

Among one of his accounts, I retained one in particular: "A man being escorted to be shot must always have his hands bound behind him. We used wire for this purpose, it's safer than rope. You let him go ahead and then follow him, commanding "to the left," "to the right," "down the stairs," etc. until he reaches the place where some sawdust or sand has been spread on the floor by the cleaning lady. And then, with the barrel close to the nape of his head without touching it though so that he is not conscious of what's going on, you pull the trigger and, at the same time, give him a mighty kick in the ass." "Why the kick?" I asked him, surprised. "Well, to prevent his blood from splashing my tunic and to spare my poor wife from having to wash it over and over again."

DORJI

Dorji only speaks Kalmuck, his people's language. He seems to be totally unaware of (and he does quite well without it!) the language of the Russian invaders who wish to impose their lifestyle upon the Kalmucks, just as they had already imposed their Cyrillic alphabet on them.

From the moment he wakes up until the moment he goes to sleep, that is from 6:00 am until 10:00 pm, he mumbles his prayers while folding his fingers. When he was arrested the Russians removed his prayer beads and his prayer wheel, two essential attributes of any good Buddhist. They also took away his clippers, so that when he is not praying Dori is plucking out his beard with his hard yellow fingernails. For hours on end he paces the five steps from the cell door to the window in the twenty inch wide passage between our two berths which are screwed onto opposite walls from each other. Sometimes he sits down to give me a turn to pace the same five steps. His lips never stop muttering his prayers.

Every time I try to talk to him in Russian, because I don't speak Kalmuck, he appears to understand nothing. His look becomes suspicious. It's as if an invisible wall was erected inside our minuscule cell in addition to those quite real ones that the NKVD has been building around me for years. How can I cross this new barrier?

In the air I draw the two humps of an Asian camel and I say, "Temen." In Dorji's eyes a spark goes off. Then I "ride on horseback," I "use the whip," and I say "Mori." I lower my head and with my fingers make horns, "Bouha." Dorji's stone face lit up in a warm smile. The few scraps of Mongol that stayed with me from when I studied oriental languages have finally come in handy. I knew that Mongol was similar to Kalmuck and in any case Dorji understood.

Now, instead of the mournful silence of before, come some animated discussions... very limited, of course, given the meager extent of my Mongol vocabulary, a language that still must be quite different from Kalmuck. As a result of this, Dorji begins to understand Russian better and actually muddles his way along fairly well. This is how I came to know that his father had spent some time in Tibet. "Did you hear him say: *O Ma ni pad mé hun?*"

Dorji's eyes lit up. So using our glutinous rye bread – all pencils and papers are strictly forbidden – I form the Tibetan letters that make up that phrase known to all Buddhist lamas.

Dorji looks at the letters, says nothing, then all of a sudden asks, "Have you seen the Dalai-Lama?" "No!" He continues to daydream. I give him my most thorough rendition of the impressive Potola palace.

In spite of its shortcomings, our conversation becomes more and more heartfelt, and I find out why Dorji is here. For centuries the Caspian steppes on either side of the Volga River had been home to the nomadic Kalmuck shepherds. By the sixteenth century, Ivan the Terrible had conquered this land known as the Golden Horde. For generations, the Russians who travelled down the Volga only settled on the riverbanks, not bothering the Kalmucks. However, under the Soviets, the colonization and russification became more oppressive. The forced collectivization imposed by Moscow in the beginning of the 1930s ruined a flourishing economy, and destroyed ancient traditions. To reinforce their hold, the Russian Communists created an "Autonomous Republic" of Kalmuckia, whose government could not contain their praise for each and every one of Moscow's initiatives. When Hitler invaded Russia, the Kalmucks knew nothing about him beyond that he was the mortal enemy of their sworn enemy. A large number of them then decided to join the German troops. In 1943 soon after the Russians had retaken the territory, Moscow decided to simply liquidate the Republic of Kalmuckia. (Five other republics suffered the same fate.) One night the entire population – several hundred thousand people – were loaded up and transported some three thousand kilometers away to the northeast to Siberia and Kazakhstan. Dorji's wife found herself in Kazakhstan with their two daughters, while Dorji ended up with his son on the shores of the Yenisei, sixteen hundred kilometers further north. His efforts to reunite with his family had all been in vain, but it did give him some notoriety, so that the authorities discovered that under the occupation, the Germans had requisitioned him as a workman.

Many years later, in 1950, here he is in my cell awaiting judgment. Upon the mere decision of the *troika* (1), he was condemned to twenty-five years of forced labor for collaboration with the enemy.

O Ma ni pad mé hum.

NOTES

(1) Composed of a three-member board, this committee is an organ of the State Security Police at the district level, empowered to levy extrajudicial settlements in absentia. The *troikas* operated from 1918 to 1953. They comprised the district party committee secretary, assisted by the head of the State Security Police and the prosecutor. Files were in the hands of the State Security Police.

Sometimes *special troikas* or *death troikas* were commissioned by the camp administration of the Gulag to shoot some categories of prisoners.

MAJOR TCHOUVACHOV, PROTECTOR OF THE SCIENCES

In 1956, twenty years after a trial that made a big stir and a sentence for high treason followed by a duly staged execution, Minister N. was rehabilitated posthumously by order of the Executive Committee of the party who thought that this was a useful step in view of new circumstances. However, in 1937, this same party thought it useful to instigate a massive reign of terror as a response to the situation of the time. It was, so it seemed, the safest way to impose the regime. The case of Minister N. was only one of the many fabricated trials of that period, called euphemistically ever since "the age of the cult of personality."

The case of Minister N. initiated a series of other trials, one of which was that of Prof. Iossef Markov who was convicted and executed as he should have been. In Russian, there is a name for the diabolical chain-reaction of numerous trials unleashed by the trial of a prominent figure: "the tail." Indeed, the process is much like a comet's tail that is full and bright near the beginning, but spreads out like a fan, and dims before it disappears in space. The brighter the comet, the longer the tail.

I met Boris Markov, the son of the professor, in 1949 at the Aleksandrovka Central Penitentiary (1) in Siberia, twelve years after his sentence. He was sentenced to eight years imprisonment on the charge of being the *son of an enemy of the people*. The day his term was to expire, he was escorted into an office and his new sentence was read to him: twenty-five years of forced labor. It was the era of the Second Great Purge, the one in the years 1947-49 which sent millions of new prisoners to the Gulag, including those who received only ten years in 1937 and were just liberated. This purge was accompanied by a noticeable hardening of the penal system. This is how, following several various transfers, the two of us ended up within the thick old walls of the Aleksandrovka to be subjected to a more strenuous solitary confinement.

At the time of his arrest, Boris was a nineteen-year-old student of Mathematics. He had already had several articles published in science magazines. Ivan Loukitch, one of our cellmates and a mathematics professor in his civilian life, remembered them well. In spite of his twelve long years in the Gulag, Boris still harbored his great passion for science. How could he do this? Simply because the Gulag was created expressly to transform "human material" into a docile, dazed and putrid blob, as which one could live only for his own survival, dreaming only of appeasing the constant gnawing pangs of hunger – if only for a moment – and avoiding as much as possible the beatings, the bad treatments, and the cold. One of the purposes of the Gulag in its entirety was to serve as a socio-cultural living laboratory and form of policing, so as to monitor experiments that might create the "perfect Soviet citizen." It was a gigantic laboratory which had at its disposal millions of guinea pigs – men, women, and adolescents.

Boris would remain lost in his thoughts for a bit. He would murmur mathematical formulae and often could be seen scrawling on his palm invisible signs. (Inmates were not allowed any pen nor paper). His strange behavior alarmed several of his buddies. Maybe he'd lost his mind? Others were uncomfortable. They knew very well that failure to "denounce suspicious behavior" was in itself enough to make accomplices all those who witnessed it... There were thirty-two of us in the cell, and each one had a sentence from fifteen to twenty-five years, and for the most part for purely fictitious reasons.

One day Boris mixed some powdered toothpaste with some water, and created a sort of white ink. He used a match as a pen, and a stool became his blackboard. In no time at all he covered it with complicated mathematical formulae that no one understood. "Stop," some well-intentioned cellmate whispered, "or else you'll get another stint for anti-Soviet crime!" "He's right," added another. "How will you prove that that's not a coded subversive message?" Lo and behold, at that very moment the senior warder, Zaitsev, appeared as if by magic. Snappily, he asks Boris' first and last names – the procedure is usually last and first name, date of birth, the article regarding his code of violation, and length of his sentence. Zaitsev is the only one among all the guards who can open the door without any squeaking at all. He is also the cruelest, and most zealous of all. After a dead silence Boris answers his questions. Zaitsev writes the given answers on his pad, grabs the stool as evidence, and leaves. "My poor Boris! Let's hope that they have enough common sense to not accuse you of plotting against the Soviets," says Loukitch.

"You'll be lucky if you only get twenty days in the cooler!"

"You can't say we didn't warn you," nags another.

The following day after the distribution of the noontime soup, the cell door hatch opens. Dead silence.

"Letter M?"

"Mikailov!" answers one of the distraught cellmates whose name begins with an M.

"Any others?

"Markov," Boris calmly replies.

"First name, date of birth, article code violation, sentence term?"

The answers coincide with the information on his sheet.

"Get your belongings!"

Boris disappears with his bundle. Some cellmates press their ears to the cell door.

"No doubt they're taking him to the cooler," says Sergei. "I heard him put his mug and bowl on the ground."

"Poor guy!"

"Well, he was asking for it."

This was the subject of the conversation until the distribution of the dishwater-like soup in the evening.

They brought Boris back from the cooler after three days. In the collective *zek* (2) memory, nothing like that had ever happened before. The cooler is always for ten days, five on rare occasions. But three? "Gentlemen!" exclaimed Professor Loukitch, "Major Tchouvachov is the most generous patron of the sciences that has ever lived." Tchouvachov being the captain of State Security who had determined the punishment according to Zaitsev's report. Tchouvachov had taken the risk of being suspected of indulging a hereditary enemy of the people, as Markov's father has gone before a firing squad!

"If he was so generous, why didn't he just throw Zaitsev's report right into the trash?," objected Muller, a veteran of the International Brigades in Spain.

"Ah, these old western intellectuals, they are incorrigible," exclaimed the wise Loukitch. "They'll never understand what true socialism is. Had the major not followed up on Zaitsev's report, Zaitsev would have certainly turned him in."

NOTES

(1) *Alexandrovski tsentral*, located near Irkutsk, which already existed during the tsars and became a pre-trial prison after 1917, under the Soviet regime.

(2) This slang word for detainee goes back to the 30s, when hundreds of thousands of prisoners were herded together to dig the White Sea Baltic Canal. The camp administration designated them by the title of "soldier-detainee of the canal": *zaklioutchenny kanaloarmeïets*, abbreviated by z/k, then *zeka* and *zek* in Russian.

THE COMPLAINT

The internal rules and regulations pinned to the wall of each cell in each Soviet prison clearly stipulate that any inmate has the right to put in writing any request or complaint directed to the judicial system of either the Soviet State or the Communist Party.

Sentenced in 1937 for "counter-revolutionary" crime he never committed, Kazakov became blind during a work related accident in the camps. Quite by chance during a transfer, we were reunited in the same cell in Aleksandrovka's Central Prison. Deprived of his sight, he simply ekes out life on his berth. He would hardly speak, even with Ketov who was his bunkmate and his eyes.

One day he was stricken with colitis. Hanging onto Ketov's arm, he was taken by the warden to the camp's doctor. The latter was a young doctor who had been assigned to the penitentiary services after completing his medical studies. He consciously looked after Kasakov's colitis, and being a newcomer, he was unaware of the habits and mores regarding inmates, and naively took an interest in Kasakov's blindness. He proceeded to examine him, and as proof that he knew nothing about the arcania of penal bureaucracy, declared to him that surgery could restore his sight. Of course, such an operation would only be possible in a specialized hospital, and he didn't know if this type of hospital existed within the Gulag structure. Moreover, it was totally out of the question to treat a Gulag inmate in a civilian facility. Everyone knew that during the period of the Tsars, transfers such as these were an excuse to arrange an escape for political prisoners. "You ought to write out a request," the kind doctor suggested to Kazakov before he discharged him.

Kazakov dictated an impressive number of requests, and generally, after several months, he would receive answers. Usually the response was off topic, or he was told that he had sent it to the wrong address. Finally, the wisemen in his cell advised him to write directly to Stalin. They well knew that it would never arrive before the august and fearsome addressee, but in seeing the name on the envelope, maybe some bureaucrat would take a look at Kazakov's case.

It was as good as done. The wisemen put their shoulders to the wheel: there was a professor of Marxism-Leninism, a former commissar from the Red Army, a rabbi, a former C.E.O., an ex-diplomat, and several other deep-thinkers without titles. As soon as Kazakov gave his go-ahead , the request was written by hand, signed, and sent through the official channels.

In the following months the potential reply was our principal subject of conversation. Of course our interest faded after a year, and conversations turned elsewhere... And then, all of a sudden, the hatch opens, and the guard whispers: "Kazakov, get ready to leave." The entire cell is instantly energized. No doubt, it must be the answer to the letter. They're going to read it to him, and make him sign it on the back. Half an hour later, he is brought back into the cell, clinging to Ketov's arm. Everyone holds their breath. As soon as the guard closes the door behind him, Kazakov turns to us and recites the content of the answer from memory: "To the chief officer of Aleksandrovka Prison, Comrade Lieutenant-Colonel Solomine. Please inform inmate Kazakov, convicted for counter-revolutionary crime by... on... that his complaint about ... dated ... addressed to Comrade Stalin, Secretary General of the Central Committee of the Communist Party of the Soviet Union, and President of the Council of Ministers of the Union of Socialist Soviet Republics, after careful review, is judged unreceivable, in view of the total absence of any causative details by which to vacate or otherwise modify the verdict currently standing in his case rendered by ..., on .... This is a certified copy. Signed: Justice Ministry Lieutenant Colonel Petrenko."

THE FAITH OF THE STALINIST

Grigori Dmitrievitch, a veteran longshoreman in Odessa and a Bolshevik since 1917, believed in Lenin and Stalin the way his deceased mother believed in God.

He had had a brilliant career. In 1937, he was the head of the Political Department of the Regional Administration of the State Railroad. Then, as was the case with so many others, he was snatched by the Great Purge. His interrogators had a hard time extracting the confessions that their superiors demanded to be able to convict him as an "enemy of the people," that is to say of Stalin – this in spite of the fact that throughout his entire life he only obeyed this same Stalin, and had done so without any reservations. Grigori Dimitrievitch avowed his devotion to the Party. He had a hard shell. He resisted. It took two years, several broken teeth, and a few cracked ribs before he would be condemned to fifteen years of forced labor for his counter-revolutionary activities. His judges remained impervious to his protests of innocence. They had all always managed to drink together in the same place over the years, they had all lived in the same neighborhood reserved for the *nomenklatura*, and their wives had all bought their groceries at the same stores reserved for the elite.

There he is in a cattle car. On each side, attached to the walls are double decker wooden bunks. A little hole in the floor serves as a latrine. There are around sixty inmates. As is the case for him, all of them have been sentenced for "counter-revolutionary crimes" that they never committed. Their sentences are for ten, fifteen, or twenty years, none for fourteen, seventeen, or nineteen. They prefer round numbers. Later on Grigori found out that it was the same story in each of the other forty-four cattle cars of the convoy, around three thousand five-hundred prisoners. Almost all of them had been good Communists, just like him.

After hours and hours of waiting the train started up, but where to? High up on the wall, under the ceiling, there is a skylight. A young man climbs up to it, and then another takes a turn. We finally understand that the train is headed east. Hours go by, the window gets dark, night falls. We are in complete darkness. The train stops. Nothing happens for a while. Then the train starts up again. It's cold. Gradually we can see our ambient window or a light on it. Dawn is breaking. The train stops, then starts up again. Hours go by.

Everyone has already eaten the seven hundred grams of rye bread, and the two salted herrings that were distributed to us before the departure. The train stops again for a long time. Outside we hear steps rushing towards us, then the sound of the sliding doors opening and closing. It comes from far away. We understand that all the cars are opened then closed, one after the other. Now, they're next door. And finally, it's Grigori's car. There's the noise of the latches. The door creaks, and suddenly a square of bright daylight blinds the occupants. Their eyes gradually adjust and through the open door they see a plain. It's deserted. In the foreground several escort soldiers have their guns pointed at the detainees. Two unarmed men approach the wagon and climb in. One of them holds a mallet. He summons the prisoners to form their ranks on one side of the wagon, and with great swings of the mallet makes sure that the walls, floor and ceiling are all sound. Then, satisfied, he yells over to his buddy: "Go ahead!" It is now the other's job to escort the prisoners one by one into the area that has been "checked." He counts them as they go by and the man with the mallet gives each one a smack in the back with the mallet. He then proceeds to inspect the other end of the wagon, and ends with the distribution of the food rations: the same two salted herrings, and seven hundred grams of rye bread. The doors close. Night sets in again, and on to the next wagon.

The convoy took seventeen days. It ended at Soutchane, the base camp for the Kolyma (1) complex. Twelve thousand kilometers were covered, during which we were allowed to have twenty-eight salted herrings, and eleven kilos nine-hundred grams of rye bread. At Kolyma, Grigori Dmitrievitch will spend many days in horrendously stressful conditions assigned to the hardest forced labor. At no time would he doubt the wisdom of the great Stalin. However, he doesn't understand. He did write him. It is obvious that none of his letters – and he wrote many dozens – ever reached Stalin's hands, not even his secretary.

When I met him in 1953 at the Central Prison of Aleksandrovka in eastern Siberia, he had become an invalid due to many work related accidents. He could barely walk, he had only three teeth and his faith left. "When I found myself inside that cattle car," he admitted to me one day, "I thought that the Party had decided to send committed militants to the Far East to uncover a plot by Japanese imperialists our services had heard rumors of. To fool the Japanese organizations, the Party had – in its infinite wisdom – decided to get us there disguised as simple prisoners, and to add credibility to their effort, made us endure all the trials reserved for true enemies of the people ..."

NOTES

(1) Territory of Eastern Siberia, bigger than France, whose name comes from the river Kolyma, 1500 miles long, ending in the Arctic Ocean. The climate is most severe: the temperature drop to -55°C and lower. The prisoners – hundreds of thousands per year – were brought by sea in the flotilla of the Kolyma camp. Those forced labor camps, amongst others, have been described by Varlam Shalamov, who gives a vivid description of them in *The Kolyma Tales*.

POPAUL

We've already been riding for three days without knowing where we are going. As always. We're jammed into a "Stolypin" car, named after the minister of the interior of the latest tsar. It was him who had the brilliant idea to convert the Russian trains for the transportation of prisoners: bars were installed over the windows, and the partition walls that separated the compartments replaced with bars, and sliding doors also with bars. Two bunk beds were enough for the comfort of four prisoners. The Soviet regime made this useful innovation by extending the norms of its predecessors, i.e. it is no longer four people that are locked up in each compartment, but thirty. The upper and lower berths are joined together by planks, or rather wood panels enough for five detainees. Two more levels were added on, one at the height of the luggage racks, and another just under the ceiling. So, all in all, if counting prisoners lying on the ground, they can hold up to thirty people. There are twenty-nine of us with our heads leaning against the bars so that the guards who stroll about day and night can see our faces.

It is still very early. The sun has just risen. We've been stopped for more than an hour, but for once we're not in the open countryside. A run-down log *isba* serves as the train station. A huge plaster statue of Lenin stands alone in this desert, pointing with his tireless right index finger towards a glorious future. The red cloth banner with the slogans waves in the morning breeze.

My neighbor Popaul, an old thief, lifts up his head from under his jacket, which he uses as his sleeping blanket. From between his swollen eyelids comes a piercing stare that doesn't miss a thing. His eyes come to rest on the slogans that promise us paradise on earth as soon as we reach communism thanks to the sure guidance of the Communist Party. He whispers into my ear: "For me, I don't need to be told what to do to achieve happiness. I only need to be told where I can find a house with a little loot to swipe. Even if it's far away, I can find it all by myself."

PACK AND GO!

For several days we have been travelling to an unknown destination, somewhere in Siberia. There are twenty-six of us in our "Stolypin" compartment. The train stops at the train station in Omsk. The escort guards – armed – make us get off the train, squat down on the platform in rows of five with our hands behind our heads. Two guards diligently count us, then realize they got it wrong and start all over again. They finally order us to get up and escort us fifty meters over to a railroad freight car. As soon as the door is closed behind us, we find ourselves in complete darkness. After a bumpy half hour, the car stops. At first we hear voices, then silence for at least an hour. "Let's go!" The wagon starts up again, slows down, then stops. We hear steps, voices. Nothing happens. At last, the door opens itself. The brightness of the day blinds us all. We are in a prison courtyard surrounded by armed guards. They walk us to a room where we are completely searched. Following that, it is the showers, then another long wait before we are taken to our cells. In a few days or a few weeks they'll make us do it all over again. That's just the way things are around here.

For the time being, a few of us are locked in a temporary storage closet. Well, not actually locked in, because it is only a framed-off end of a hallway with plywood walls that don't even go up to the ceiling. The door, also made out of plywood, has just a hook on the outside. Not terribly serious for a prison! As soon as the guards are out of sight, a twelve-year old juvenile delinquent who is locked in with us, climbs up the wall like a monkey and opens the door on the other side. "Pack and go," he yells, beaming with happiness. "Everyone is free!"

It was hard to believe the look on the faces of all those "enemies of the people" who had just been amnestied by little Vassia. They were panic stricken. They were all loyal citizens who had been condemned to sentences ranging from eight to twenty years for crimes they didn't commit, and here they are, thanks to the kid Vassia, ready to infringe the rules of the Soviet administration which sentenced them – unjustly, nonetheless. Among them are a former general and two former colonels of the Red Army, all condemned for high treason; a former diplomat, a stamp collector, an Esperantist condemned for espionage (because they had been in touch with foreigners); two engineers, and a university professor condemned for sabotage; the former first violin player of the Moscow State Opera, three students, and terrorists – weren't most of the attacks against the tsar carried out by students? Here are all these "dangerous" enemies of the people begging little Vassia to immediately shut the door before the guards discover their attempt – involuntary, of course, yet real, and even collective – to escape.

Vassia, a good kid, wound up locking the odd adults back down in their makeshift cell because they turned down the liberty he so generously offered them.

THE PEASANTS

"Cut down with a scythe." A great way to describe him – that's exactly the way he looked. He must be seventy-five, or eighty years old, rugged, shorn like the rest of us. His white haired head shakes, his fingers are chubby, calloused, and the index and thumb are yellowed from years of smoking. His pale blue eyes seem to be looking into the far distance.

We are in 1940 in one of the countless forced labor camps of the Gulag's empire. The man, Nikanor, is into his ninth year. For me, it is only my third. As a young French Communist, I'm just liberating myself from the Marxist-Leninist illusions caused by the overwhelming impact of the Soviet realities that are spread out before me in the Gulag, and above all because of the thousands of biographical accounts of my fellow inmates coming from all strata of Soviet society. As for Nikanor, he is an old peasant whose parents were serfs. They were witnesses to the revolutions of 1905 and February 1917, as well as the coup d'état of October 1917. He harbors no illusions. I listen to him. He speaks very softly, in a monotone voice, with no emphasis. He just reports a long list of facts, almost like a statement. I have been listening to him for a while, dumbfounded, "The first died just one or two hours after his birth, the second held out until the following morning."

Nikonor was speaking of the twins born in 1931 in a livestock wagon. These were his great grandchildren. The wagon was one of a long convoy transporting about a hundred families of peasants thought to be *kulaks* to an unknown destination. Each of the families had had to leave as a family, with nursing babies, bedridden grandparents, and pregnant women too. Armed soldiers had surrounded the village and the commissar told the village people to gather up only the belongings that they could carry. All that they left behind – lands, buildings, livestock, furnishings, clothing, utensils, etc. – became property of the *kolkhoz*, the collective farm, and this without any compensation whatsoever.

Nikanor's story, which he told with his chronicler's droning mono-tone, made me sick. Suddenly memories came flooding back... Long before my Gulag career as a prisoner began, I was undercover oper-ating for the Comintern assigned a mission somewhere in Western Europe. The local press had published a sensational article about the collectivization of the farms in Russia. And here I was hearing the exact same thing from Nikanor! At that, I even wondered if he hadn't read the same newspapers. I recall how at that time I had utterly rejected this "abject slander directed at the number one na-tion of workers and peasants." I can even remember that some solid bourgeois could hardly believe it too, no more than world opinion in 1943 would believe the first reports on the burning Nazi crema-toriums.

I guess in some way, I contributed to all of this. It is painful to admit it, and I am still ashamed of it to this day.

STEP TO THE LEFT, STEP TO THE RIGHT...

They took one step to the left, maybe three, and it may well have been the last steps of their lives.

When escorting us from the gates of the camp to the worksite, the escort guard repeats the age-old command: "Any step to the left or to the right is considered an escape attempt. The escort will fire without warning. Understood?" And all of us answer according to regulations: "Understood!" We've all heard this warning a zillion times and the answer has become so systematic, so like an "amen" that for generations we call it "the prayer."

We are instructed to walk in ranks of five men, escorted by soldiers pointing their guns at us. A dog handler with a German shepherd makes up the tail of the procession.

We walk past a pile of bags of flour. They had been retrieved from a wrecked barge that had been refloated. Through some holes in the fabric we see some stale flour, greyish with lumps that look like pebbles. Two young prisoners can't resist the temptation, and jump for the bags. Immediately there is a gunshot, only one. Both of them fall on the ground, one squirms then stops moving. The other groans, and twitches. The column keeps on walking. According to camp regulations, no one can help them before the return of the security officer. He is away and his assistant hasn't sobered up since the night before.

Later on we found out that the bullet had gone through the spinal cord of the first man before hitting the head of the other. The rifleman – as is common practice – received eight days of paid leave, following a quick and formal inquiry.

STALIN DOES BETTER THAN CUVIER

Some thrashing noise, everything starts spinning around the barracks. Is it the end of the world? No, it's simply the noise of the doors being unlocked that pulls me out of my sleep, the supreme delight of a detainee. The crude light of the lighbulb which is never turned off – even at night – tears at my eyelids and blinds my pupils. Now that I am awake, I hear the key in the keyhole, then the squeaky noise of the door opening to let someone in that shuts almost right afterwards. The key turns again in the keyhole and the locks are pushed closed, with the bar and a big lock.

Long before the end of this long procedure the beady eyes of the newcomer have already scrutinized the overstuffed world he has been locked in. He is small and stocky and looks famished. There is something about him that reminds me of a hyena, something unusual and scary. Is he really a human being? He looks like the images of the humanoids depicted in the natural history posters that used to cover the walls of the school I attended in another life. It is the first time in ten years in the Gulag that I find myself facing a Neanderthal! I get a chill.

Without a word, the Neanderthal sits on the berth below. I am on the upper one. Those berths are sixty centimetres wide and three metres seventy long, sleeping two men. They take half of the cell which is one metre twenty out of four metres long. In the corner, by the door, there is a sticky and stinky latrine bucket.

The Neanderthal remains silent. I am staring at him and an idea crosses my mind: Cuvier became famous worldwide because of his idea of recreating an antediluvian animal from a single bone. Our genius Stalin – right in the middle of the 20th century – created such conditions that he was able to bring some cavemen back to life! This amazing discovery doesn't keep me awake, yet I have no time to go back to sleep because I am awakened by another thrashing noise, the metal bar, the lock and the key in the door. Here comes another specimen, for sure, taller than the former one. He lies next to the other one. They start whispering. I strain my ear. Again, more screeching noises by the door. A third critter is brought in who goes and sits by the other two. More whispers until a hand pulls me by the leg, "Hey, you pigeon, you go and lie down below!" I immediately obey, grouchily. The first caveman and his tall friend climb up to the upper berth while the third one remains on the one below, with his head leaning against the wall opposite the door. I have the choice between having my head at his feet or near the latrine bucket. I am both furious and helpless, and do my best to go back to sleep. Years in the Gulag have taught me not to fight with an enemy obviously stronger than me. Like the old Russian saying goes: "Do not sue someone who is wealthier than you, nor try to fight with someone stronger."

I hear the two companions devouring the bread I had saved. I am half awake when the door opens again. The guard takes me out of the cell and puts me in the hands of the 'stroller,' i.e. the escort guard in charge of escorting inmates inside the compound. In fact, he doesn't 'take them for a stroll,' he orders them to walk in front of him, and gives them commands, "To the right! To the left! Continue forward!" He has me go through several corridors and hallways, and climb up some staircases. I have become an old hand at this, just like the padded door in front of which he orders me to stop. "Halt! Face the wall!" He knocks at the door, waits for a response and says, "Comrade Sergeant, the inmate is yours!"

Commissar-Interrogator Arseniev, behind his desk, signs the entry form that the 'stroller' proffers. Before that he looks at this watch and checks the time. The smoke coming from his cigarette butt dangling at the corner of his mouth makes him squint his left eye. The 'stroller' takes back the form, bows and then leaves the room. The commissar leans back in his seat, takes a puff and looks at the clouds of smoke until he notices me. Briskly, he asks me to take a seat – not in front of him, but on a stool screwed to the floor in one of the most remote corners of the room. The regulations require that the inmate stay seated facing straight ahead, with his legs tight and his hands on his knees.

He remains silent for a while, holding his chin in his right hand, staring around. Then all of a sudden, his fingers keep moving and he drops his cigarette. I hear it fall on the ground. As if he had been awakened abruptly, he turns to me and says, "It must have been difficult for you to be in solitary confinement for eleven months – now you have company."

There is some warmth in his voice. He then pauses and lectures me about the customs of cannibals. He is not talking about some remote tribe from Siberia but precisely about my new cellmates. It turns out that they have eaten human flesh. On their last escape, since they were running out of food supplies, they shot the fourth man of the group and ate him.

I knew of this phenomenon, but still I found it difficult to believe. Wasn't it some tale? Well, here is a most official representative briefing me with many details about the procedure. What shocks me the most is not so much the monstruous facts but his nonchalant, almost blasé tone of voice. He could have been a traveller recounting his impressions from his voyages in some exotic land. This whole thing reminds me of an old English gentleman I had known in my childhood, at the end of WWI. He would spend his holidays in a villa next to ours, and was often invited for tea at our house where he would tell us about his African adventures. He had been an explorer as a young man in the 19th century. Our household was just fascinated by his unusual tales. I was probably six or seven years old but I have vivid recollections of him telling us about his encounter with a tribe of cannibals and of how terrified I was. I can still hear the amused and blasé voice of this old colonial man speaking of "colored men," those "savages" he considered inferior... while the Soviet Arseniev talks about his people, his fellow countrymen.

After this most detailed lecture about man-eaters, he then turns to serious matters: I am being accused of espionage on behalf of the French, British and American governments – my accomplices – and carrying this out from this remote camp, located on the edge of the Arctic Pole.

It's painful and very long, until someone knocks at the door. It's the 'stroller.' What a relief! It's over, at least for now. The commissar after checking his watch signs the entry form and gives it to the stroller. "Hands behind your back! Keep on walking!" He immediately follows me. "To the left! To the right!" The same old commands. We arrive at the pre-trial prison. Bread is being distributed, a sign that it must be after 6:00 am. The regulations prohibit detainees from lying down and resting during the day until 10:00 pm, otherwise they are sent to jail; same thing if someone is caught sitting down, with his eyes closed. Some can sleep that way. I can barely stand on my feet. "Hey, didn't you have fun, man?" asks the tallest of my new cellmates as soon as the door is closed. I don't answer. I am thirsty, and fortunately there is still some water in my bowl. I drink it all. "Here, you still have some sugar left. Take it. It'll give you some strength." For some obscure reason, my three companions haven't gobbled my sugar. I accept their generous offer without trying to understand. The tallest continues: "You know that before we got transferred here, the senior warder promised us fifty grams of tobacco if we agreed to knock off a rebel the guards couldn't handle." The three men are not aggressive with me.

One or two hours later they are marched from the cell. They didn't get their tobacco. They intentionally and generously forgot about it.

SHORTCUTS

In Norilsk, the escort who would takes us to work on the compound makes us cross a railway. Along the rails we often see cranes, bags, and various gear waiting to be picked up by the intended recipients. Sometimes there are bags neatly lined up, and some that are filled with sawdust and straw are to be used as mattresses for convicts. Today they look bizarre: they are smaller than usual, tied up with a knot and obviously contain something else than straw. On one end at the bottom, there's what looks like a watermelon in the shape of a sphere. Our escort walks by, without noticing anything. I ask the man who walks next to me, "What can these bags possibly hold?" My ignorance seems to surprise him and even raise some suspicion, something that surprises me too. Later I will learn that not only are there "un-persons" in this Orwellian world, but there are indeed "un-facts," "un-events," and "un-phenomena" in the Socialist empire. Thus, everyone knows about these things but they have to pretend they ignore them, and any question asked is perceived as a trick so that the man looks at me and tells me reassuringly, "These are 'souvenirs from Kalargon.'" I don't get it. "Well, those bags contain beheaded bodies and what looks like a watermelon is the head.

"But what is this Kalargon where they have their heads chopped off?" "It is the punitive section where the criminals, the hardened ones, are transferred. According to their traditions, they settle their matters among themselves and chop off the offender's head. Before they bury the prisoner, instructions are that his body must be clearly identified and a tag with his file number be tied to his left toe. If the corpse has been butchered, regulation states that each piece must be identified, something only possible in Norilsk where all the central files are stored with all the prisoners' data from all the compounds of the labor camp."

Later on I found out the hard way that sometimes the camp officer may resort to transferring political prisoners to Kalargon if they think that "rehabilitation through labor" is too slow, or even impossible – that very rehabilitation which is the main objective of the Gulag. And sometimes thugs belonging to hostile gangs are sent there, thus giving the local administration some respite.

ALBINAS

Albinas was fourteen years old when we met in Siberia, in the huge Krasnoyarsk transit prison. He had been sentenced to ten years of forced labor for "banditry." It was in 1949, a time when Lithuania was still resisting the Soviet invader.

He told me that a unit of Red Army soldiers had arrived at their farm in Lithuania carrying a cart on which one could see a long, still shape covered under a blanket. An officer had stepped right into the farm, followed by three armed soldiers. "Where is the old man?" he asked the mother. She looked at him, pale as a sheet, incapable of uttering a word. Without getting cross, the lieutenant insisted. "I not know… He go away… Far," the mother mumbled in her broken Russian. Four little children, their eyes opened wide with fright, cling to their mother's skirt. Niiolé, Albinas's twelve-year-old sister, snuggles in her brother's arms. There is silence until the officer yells, "Something to drink!" The mother doesn't understand. "Vodka!" he shouts. That's a word that every Lithuanian would understand. She goes into the next room with the four kids, and comes back alone, a bottle in her hand. The Russians start drinking. They become very happy. The officer barks an order. Two soldiers leave the room, take from the cart what is obviously a corpse, come back with it and lay it on the dining room table. The officer pulls out the blanket and says, "Say hi to your husband." Albinas sees a brain turned to mush, fragments of bones, and blood. That's all that's left of a face, and indeed it's his father's. Haggard, the mother looks without seeing. A Russian takes a harmonica out of his pocket. The bouncy notes of a Cossack tune fill the room. The soldiers search the house and find more vodka. "Dance!' commands the lieutenant. The mother stands still, lost in her thoughts. He pulls out a revolver, aims at the ceiling, then points the gun at little Niiolé. "*Iob tvoïou mat!* Dance, you sons of a bitches!" Albinas cannot remember how long they danced, all three of them, he, his mother and Niiolé. Then they were all put together onto the cart with the father's corpse.

Some time later they were judged and sentenced; it only took two seconds and a few stamps. Little Niiolé was sentenced to five years of forced labor and he, Albinas, ten years; the mother twenty, and all three of them for banditry.

SOME FINE PSYCHOLOGISTS

The thug is perspicacious: with a glance he can figure out whom he's dealing with.

One day at the very beginning of my career in the Gulag, I was transferred to another team and I had to change barracks and get my bread ration from another person in charge. When I appeared in front of him, I introduced myself, "My name is Rossi, Jacques, and I have been assigned here. I was told you are the one who gives me my bread ration."

Later on I would find out that that this hoodlum responsible for the bread ration was a seasoned thug, which did not surprise me, as thugs always find a way to get themselves this type of cushy position, real hideaways. Right away he gave me my allotment of bread without any questions.

At that time I was still quite naive, and I found nothing abnormal in what had happened. It was only later as I was learning about life (and the Gulag is a heck of a school for that) that I asked myself several questions. How could an orderly deliver a bread ration as easily as he had—something that is so coveted—to someone whom he had just seen for the first time? So one day I just came out and asked him. "You know, I've got a flair," he said to me. "I can sniff people out right away. I could tell you were just a pigeon, and even a "pigeon's pigeon," surely someone who wouldn't be stupid enough to claim a bread ration he wasn't entitled to."

Another good example of this exceptional flair happened at the beginning of my stay in the Gulag. I clumsily attempted to rid myself of my culture like a chick hatching out of an egg. It was in Doudinka (1), on the shores of the Yenisei. We were a team of *zeks*, pushing a bulk load of tree trunks towards the railroad tracks. Two teams of *zeks* worked across from one another, separated by this pile of logs. We were to load the tree trunks onto a platform using only pike poles with hooks on the ends. The more the pile dwindled, the closer the teams got to each other. The team across from me was made up entirely of hoodlums. One of them wouldn't stop insulting me, and he was threatening me with his pike pole. I didn't take the bait. I had risked my life in Spain for the good of mankind, I wasn't going to let myself be intimidated by this piece of society's garbage—which he certainly was, since, after all, he was here in the Gulag. For me, of course, it was a different story, it was a mistake!

When he arrived right in front of me, he looked me straight in the eye and said, "You're not a dog. You have the eyes of a human being." He then put down his pike, and the incident was over. Later on some of my buddies gave me an explanation of his behavior and it was all because of my hat. In Moscow when we were transferred from Butyrka Prison to the camps, the inmates who had no clothes could buy old ones from the camp administration. At the time of my arrest, I was wearing an old Parisian felt hat. One of my fellow inmates said with a chuckle that he thought that it would be a bit incongruous where I was going, so he very generously bought me a superb dark blue *chapka* with yellow lining. It was a dubious gift because, as I was to find out later, it was a *chapka* formerly worn by the police. Evidently my hoodlum friend thought that I was an ex-police officer, but on closer inspection it was clear to him that I had none of the attributes of one.

It goes without saying that a thug really knows right away who he is dealing with. It goes with the profession. For him, it is often a matter of life or death.

NOTES
(1) An old fishing village, which became a maritime and fluvial port city, at the mouth of the Yenisei beyond the Arctic Circle. From the early 30s, labor, goods and equipment intended for the Norilsk camp were shipped from Doudinka. Between 1930 and 1960 it was regarded as a section of the camp.

SAVOIR-VIVRE

Grichka, Michka and Sachka were fun and nice. All three of them were young delinquents, and they happened to be my neighbours in my barracks. We were part of the same team. Together we learned to cheat at work by practising *toufta* (1). They would often ask me to recount anecdotes of when I lived abroad. For them there were only two countries: the Soviet Union, and 'Abroad,' some myterious, promising, fairy tale land. So I did my best recounting anecdotes.

One day on the worksite they managed to find me a plate full of *kasha*, that porridge which is the staple food of the Russian people. There was only one spoon. As a sign of friendship they offered me the first bite. The spoon was then handed on to the next person, and so on. The offer had put me ill-at-ease because there was no water to wash the spoon. As a novice, having no idea of proper manners in a forced labor camp, instead of licking the spoon so that it shone like a new penny I did my best to avoid touching it with my lips and when I thought I had had my share, I became very embarrassed and passed the collective tool to Grichka with a little semolina left on it. The latter confessed to me later that he was most surprised to see such an 'educated' person like me—since I was a foreigner and spoke several languages—behave in such a vulgar way. It took me a while to adapt to the rules of Gulag *savoir-vivre*.

Another example of that lack of good manners found amongst the newcomers: it took place in the transit prison of Krasnoiarsk in 1948. There were about twenty of us, some foreigners, all in a cell. Most of us ignored our final destination, except for Engineer N., some big name in the steel industry who was sought after by the industrial complex of Norilsk.

The door opens letting in a newcomer, some stout guy, exuding self-confidence who doesn't look like a thug but rather a *moujik* (2). He says "good morning" without even waiting for the door to close behind him. He's got some *savoir-vivre*! He heads out to one of the tables available, puts his belongings on it, takes out his snuff box and pours a little bit of tobacco on the table. "Why don't you roll yourselves one?" he says simply. The audience cannot believe their ears. For some, tobacco is even more precious than bread. Everyone tries to remain dignified and not rush all at once. That takes some considerable effort. All of a sudden, there is one who marches straight to the table, heading for the precious heap—if looks could kill! He opens his own snuff box which he starts filling, pinch by pinch, half way up with the tobacco from the rich donor. He then leans toward him and says with a strong German accent: "*Spassiba!*" It was General von und Zu., a distinguished and cultured German aristocrat.

NOTES

(1) Lying, cheating, forgery. The term *tufta* appeared for the first time in the 1920s in the speech of recidivist criminals. It comes from the acronym TFT, *Tiajoly Fizitcheski Troud*, i.e. Heavy Manual Labor which later became *Tecknika Ucheta Fiktivnogo TrudaI*, i.e. Technique of Accounting for Fictitious Labor. The term deals with a concept to understand the essence of the Soviet regime and its economy. Marxist-Leninist ideals being unachievable, and since Stalin had claimed that this utopia to be a reality, the whole country had to resort to *tufta*, i.e. lying to validate the lies of the leaders of the party.

(2) Russian word for peasant which became in many foreign languages the equivalent of "the coarse Russian peasant with a beard."

THE COW

Everything is white : the tundra, the sky and the horizon. There are six *zeks* in our party escorted by two guards. We are following three topographical engineers. They tread with much difficulty through the deep snow. We are there to carry their equipment—theodolite, notebooks, and stakes. It's simple. The escorts are not pressing at our heels. It almost seems that we're on vacation... What a treat!

"What in the world is that?" ask Artchil. Far off in the vast whiteness, he makes out a grey speck. He is sure. I squint my eyes, but I can't see anything. As we draw near, the others start noticing something too. It looks like a stump. Everyone, surveyors, escorts, inmates keep their eyes riveted on that enigmatic object. "It's odd; it looks like a seated man," said one of the engineers. "Yeah, and he's absolutely still," remarks another one, surprised. "What the hell would he be doing way out here in the midst of this frozen desert?"—"It's a cow," comments my neighbor.

In fact, it is indeed a man. The arrival of our little group doesn't seem to trouble him. He remains seated, completely still. His feet disappear in the snow, his arms are around his knees, and by the look of his clothing, he could only be an inmate. He looks very young. Without saying a word, one of the guards walks up to him and pushes him over with the butt of his gun. The man, still motionless, topples over without unfolding his arms. He must have been dead for quite some time. The soldier leans over him. Without removing his mitten, he pushes aside the dead man's red and green scarf. On each side of his neck there is an incision in the artery. The soldier puts the dead man back upright, and checks his kidneys. The jacket cracks, like a shell of ice. We can see two gaping wounds at the kidneys. He's a "cow."

Another word for it is "ram" or "luggage." All these terms are associated with food supplies for the road, or—to be more accurate—he whose blood and kidneys are to be eaten still warm, by his comrades, if for any reason during the course of an escape they find themselves short of food. The seasoned thugs delegate this task to a young inmate who has no idea what is in store for him, and who is only too proud to be included in an escape attempt with the hardest criminals of the camp. Sometimes things go well, and the novice— the "cow"—will realize only much later the risk he has taken. Maybe then will he appreciate the humour of those who advised him to bring along some salt. It is dangerous during an escape to light a fire for fear that you'll be spotted, therefore, the only two parts of the "cow"—the blood and the kidneys—can be drunk and eaten raw... and it goes down easier with a little bit of salt.

Our formation continues its route. Suddenly it hits me: I know that boy! It was a year ago. I had just arrived in the camp. He was barely fifteen, very naive. He had no idea why he was there and pleaded innocent. He had asked me to write a letter of request on his behalf and as a token of gratitude wanted to give me the green and red scarf that his mother had knitted for him.

I can't figure out why those who ate this "cow" left the scarf. In any case it was certainly their sense of humor that had them sit the corpse upright when it would have been easier just to leave it where it lie. Thugs love practical jokes.

THE BET

They had just delivered to our cell the items that had been ordered from the prison canteen by our "privileged ones," i.e. those who receive packages from their families. Like anywhere else, the poor outnumber the few privileged ones. Here you can tell them apart at a glance, those who have rounded features and the others with emaciated faces, empty bellies, visible ribs, and an attitude that can sometimes be excessively humble and sometimes most agressive.

On the table a pile of bread, some cheap tobacco, sugar, onions and other marvellous things are laid out. The "canteen commission"—two or three men selected by the privileged ones—are busy sharing and distributing the orders. Serious and concentrated on their tasks, they look like priests celebrating mass. The privileged wait patiently, with much respect and dignity, knowing that the celebration can only be to their benefit. As for the poor, some cannot take their eyes off the mesmerizing show that makes their mouths drool. Others pretend they're not looking, yet don't miss a thing. Last, there are the ones who know how to not look or see.

Tradition has it that about one tenth of the order that each privileged person receives is distributed amongst the poor. The commission handles it and shares this manna between the beneficiaries.

Veterinarian Averianov, a tall and disheveled figure, was the most famished looking of our poor cellmates. When the question "how much bread can a man eat in one shot?" was asked randomly, he answered immediately, "Four kilos." This is one of the most recurring questions in camps and prisons. There have been many rumors and myths about it, with great detail, but four kilos, wow! "Without drinking?" asks another naive starving wretch. "Without drinking!," says Averianov, steadfastly. "Prove it!" says another one. They take bets and form two teams. "Will we be able to collect four kilos of bread?" asks Frolov provocatively, a privileged one who pretends to be generous. "Here's half a kilo to kick off." Some of the rest answer the call but without much enthusiasm. "Come on, cut it out! Don't you see?" protests Mikhael Grigorievitch. "If you make him keep his bet, you are going to kill him." The show goes on. The four kilos, or rather what makes up about four kilos, are gathered. There is no scale, so they choose old man Batov to do the slicing. He has had more than twenty years in the Gulag and is able to gauge bread rations down to five grams.

Surrounded by a group of fans, Averianov beams with happiness. After so many years he is going to be able to eat his fill! Everyone gives him their insights and hints. Some quote famous people. He promises himself that he will take his time. But it's all too much to resist. The first enormous mouthfuls go down in a blink of an eye. He starts again. He is more serious, he chews conscientiously. He becomes more and more serious. His jaw moves more and more slowly. His buddies follow each step of the process as though it were a game. You can see that he is beginning to flag. His eyes look worried. He turns white as a sheet. Large beads of sweat form on his forehead. Some of his companions say that he should give up. Others encourage him. He continues. Finally his jaw no longer does what he wants it to do. He cannot get the last mouthful down. He is shattered. There are only two hundred grams to go. Someone touches his forehead. "Oh shit! He's burning hot!" Other hands reach out to touch him. Grichka knocks on the door, someone goes to get the nurse. He doesn't get there till an hour later, takes Averianov's temperature, looks at the column of mercury and leaves. Two hours go by. They escort Averianov out "with all his stuff"—that means that he is to be transferred somewhere else.

Two years later I found myself in the same cell as an inmate who shared his room with Averianov in the medical unit. The poor wretch had died within a few hours.

It is uncertain that the purveyors of those fatal four kilos of bread wanted to have fun at the expense of the famished Averianov. Maybe they were afraid of being called stingy.

A GOOD JOKE

Alois the Austrian had been living for at least three years in the same barracks with a bunch of hoodlums, all with cushy jobs. Having picked up a working knowledge of Russian, this hoodlum wannabe had been head of the barracks. In other words, it was he who went to fetch the hot water and bread rations, and also maintained good order in the barracks. All of these were light-duty tasks. Even if occasionally he had to accept a difficult chore, he was nonetheless still his own boss and no one was there looking over his shoulder.

Grisha was a hoodlum, and like any hoodlum he was feared. His appearance did nothing to hide his lineage: he had a particularly gravelly deep voice, a complexion scattered with smallpox marks and other scars, a row of steel teeth, red hair and a long scar on his forehead.

Broken-Nose was also a hoodlum. He had been chosen to guard a stock of food supplies, a position the camp administration gave intentionally to those who came from the criminal underworld because no one was better trained than them to see through the scams of prospective thieves. And when they would help themselves, it was with the consent and complicity of the officer in command.

Broken-Nose was big, well built, and rather quiet. He was polite, like hoodlums can be, and used the formal form of address to everyone except his closest friends. Above all, he had a great sense of humor.

We found ourselves in a section of the camp that surprisingly contained both men's and women's barracks. Grisha "had a woman." One day, just for fun, Broken-Nose bet him that he would screw his Macha. Grisha was fully aware of the terror that he inspired not only within his circle, but also within the heart of blond and frail Macha with her rosy cheeks. Because of this, he was sure that she wouldn't possibly be unfaithful to him. Yet Broken-Nose knew how to take full advantage of his work assignment and was able to barter some food supplies for some women's clothings and, in that way, lure Macha over to his barrack.

"Listen, buddy," he then said to Alois. "Macha, Grisha's woman, is coming over here to screw me. I want you to hold a sheet in front of my bunk to give us some privacy and get a pail of cold water ready near the doorway with some chunks of ice in it. As soon as I'm done, I'll get out of here immediately, and you will remove the sheet and throw the pail of water between her legs." As planned, Alois was nimble and threw the icy bucket at the exact time and location. Macha was instantly stricken with horror and bolted out of the bunk as fast as her legs would carry her. So fast, in fact, that she forgot the pretty shoes that her sweet Grisha had given her. This was exactly what Broken-Nose needed to prove to Grisha what had gone on, and that he had indeed won the bet: a half-liter of 95° alcohol that the two would empty together.

Macha was most fortunate, Grisha didn't kill her. He settled for a good beating and she got out of it with a couple of weeks in the hospital.

BETWEEN THUGS

The camp administration was no longer able to put an end to the bloody vendetta killings that were happening between the rival gangs. Every day there were deaths, and this reduced the available stock of human capital, especially since there wouldn't be any newcomers for six months, until the Yenisei lost its icy shell. Furthermore, the killings spread panic amongst the other inmates. The hoods, the hardened hoods, put up such a savage resistance to the administration's effort to get them to work, that only the other inmates, the pigeons, ended up working. In short, this state of affairs jeopardized the completion of the "plan," and consequently the bonuses that the bureaucrats would receive if they exceeded it.

The camp administration therefore took the initiative to separate the two enemy factions by dividing the camp with a "free-fire zone." It was a strip of land about one-and-a-half meters wide with strands of barbed wire on each side. Armed guards, perched in their watchtowers, were to fire without warning upon anyone with the unfortunate luck to venture too close to it. Because of this measure, the deaths substantially subsided.

However, the dominant gang refused to have anything to do with this imposed truce. One of them had the bright idea of digging a tunnel through the three-foot thick shell of ice that had covered the ground now for at least three months. This is a difficult and technically demanding task. Nevertheless, they managed. Yet before undertaking an assault on the enemy camp to slit their throats while they sleep, they decided that they must scout out the premises. They had to locate the bunks of Broken-Tooth Ivan, Crater-Face Grisha, Black Ass Abderrahman, and the other most dangerous gang members.

So one night with the wind and snow swirling around, Sacha, the chosen scout, sneaks into the enemy's barracks. The great majority of the inhabitants are merely convicts. There are only about ten hoodlums. Sacha infiltrates the inmates and finds a spot on the lower bunk near the door. He goes to sleep just like everyone else with his woolen hat pulled down over his eyes, against the cold. From his bunk he can see everything without being discovered. But then....

"Wanna eat a nice plate of warm food?" asks a friendly voice. Someone taps him gently on the shoulder. "You must be freezing and starving, you poor guy!" Sacha grows pale. His mind is racing. How could he escape his impending cruel death. Very kindly the man motions to Sacha to come sit in the hoods' corner by the wood stove. A steaming pot is waiting there for him. How could he pretend that he is not hungry? Inmates are always starving, as opposed to the hoodlums who are the leaders and don't need to work—they make the others work.

Not knowing what to say, Sacha gives in and decides to play along with them. He gets up and follows the man. After all, it could happen that hoodlums may commit purely generous acts. He makes himself eat. His guests show much compassion and commiseration for the poor inmate that he is, who has just completed a hard day's work. One of them even offers him a big chunk of sugar and another gives him a full ration of bread.

"Micha, spark up the fire!" orders Crater-Face Grisha. "This poor guy's freezing!"

They ask him questions, they feel sorry for him. "Hey! By the way, who's your boss?"

Sacha mumbles something. Other questions become more and more confrontational. During this time Micha is hugging the stove. The thick iron plate that covers it becomes purple, then cherry-red, then white-hot. One of the hoods starts playing the balalaika, and the others join in singing at the top of their lungs.

The cat and mouse game is over. Two henchmen grab Sacha's arms and tie them behind his back with barbed wire, the same with his feet. All of a sudden he is thrown on top of the stove. His clothing bursts into flames, he screams bloody murder, moans. There is the putrid odor of burning flesh. The chorus and balalaika get louder, but you can still hear the terrifying howls. Finally they slow down, and when it seems that it's over, one more pitiful cry tears the air. The musicians are out of breath. The stench is unbearable. The hoods open the door, and break the windowpanes, even though it is 25°Celsius below zero. The two-hundred other inmates of the barracks pretend to be sleeping. They know that the cost of witnessing the actions of the hoods could be their life. When I raise my head to peek, the enormous hand of my neighbour Petro slams my head back down. He says nothing. It isn't until the next day that he recites for me one of the prime commandments of the Gulag: "See nothing, hear nothing, say nothing." He has known and internalized this for a long time. It was drummed into him at the *kolkhoz* and then later when he did his military service in the Red Army. "They didn't teach you that in your university, did they?" he asks with a broad smile.

THE INFORMER'S PAYCHECK

His buddies had fleeced him when they were divying up the booty. He turned them in to the commissar who, as a reward, had asked the work assigner to assign Tolia on less strenuous, and if possible more "calorific" duties that would thus enable him to steal a bit of food. The work assigner never liked the commissar's favorites. They were generally lazy, but what could he do? He too was scared. So Tolia was assigned to the bakery as a sweeper. However, it didn't take long for the *zeks* of the bakery to figure out what type of "favors" Tolia was doing for the commissar. They arranged amongst themselves to have Tolia caught with his hand in the cookie jar, so that he would inevitably be sent to solitary confinement. Then, he was assigned to do heavy construction work. It was gruelling. Nevertheless, in the meantime Tolia had performed several favors "satisfactorily," and as a result, the Commissar assigned him to the dispensary. There, once again, his fellow workers quickly caught on to his subterfuge and got rid of him quickly. Again, Tolia found himself assigned to the "regular" construction work. And, one more time he went to plead favors from the commissar. By then, the latter realized that Tolia was useless and that all the inmates knew that he was a stoolie so he deliberately transferred him to the section of the camp where those he had turned in were serving their sentences.

The next morning they found Tolia's severed head lying by the latrine bucket. This is in keeping with the hardened criminal's code. The commissar knew exactly what was going to happen and thus neatly got rid of an informer who was no longer useful to him. He won't have any trouble finding another one amongst all the starving inmates.

As a conscientious bureaucrat, he opened an inquiry regarding Tolia's murderers; he "smoked them out," and arrested them. He got depositions from the witnesses, and complete confessions from the guilty parties. Then he sent the case file to the judges. All this was very neatly orchestrated because the inquiry, the trial and the prosecution were all handled by one and the same person.

Tolia's murderers, some old recidivists, were sentenced to another ten years for premeditated murder. Justice had been served.

PAID LEAVE

Broken-Tooth is sick of it. Sick of everything, sick of the punitive section of Kalargon where the men on duty beat him up each time he refuses to go to work in the quarries, the only worksite in the area. These men here are all hoodlums, just like him, except that they are members of the rival gang, they are all "bitches" (1), while he prides himself on being an "honest" thug, "a true one." Ah! If only he were with the "true" guys, there wouldn't be any problems.

It has already been several months that he has been in Kalargon. How much longer will they let him just rot here? And furthermore, winter is almost here; working in the open-air quarries with a temperature of forty-five degrees Celsius below zero, no thanks!

"Death to Stalin! Down with the Soviets!" he would yell as soon as he sees the commissar. The latter doesn't even react nor turn around. Normally an outburst like this would immediately get this dangerous "terrorist" clapped into the cooler, but the commissar knows that Broken-Tooth is an inveterate recidivist criminal and no danger at all to the Soviet state. He only wants to be transferred to a pre-trial prison. Inmates awaiting their sentences are not forced to work. The rations allowed for these inmates is four-hundred grams of bread, and nine grams of sugar per day whereas a normal inmate who refuses to work is only allotted three-hundred grams of bread and no sugar. It is therefore a good deal to be sentenced. The commissar, however, doesn't want to play Broken-Tooth's game. So the only way for him to get what he wants is to fall back on the old classic method, i.e. to murder a fellow inmate, any inmate, the first to fall within his grasp. No sooner said than done, and poof! There he is in pre-trial prison. He is clever enough to make the investigation drag on until the spring, and make sure that in the meantime no one tries to make him work.

Of course after his trial he'll be sent back to a camp with a new sentence of from five to eight years. He will have enjoyed a "paid leave" of five or six months. After all, the Gulag for him and his peers is like the factory, or the office for the rest of us... just a normal routine.

NOTES

(1) Turncoat thieves or traitors i.e. those who the "true thieves" do not consider as part of their brotherhood. As a matter of fact, they would violate their laws which forbid any cooperation with the camp administration or authorities, including turning in another inmate, be it a stoolie. There is a number of testimonies from authors who spent time in the Gulag about the bloody wars fought between the "Bitches" and the "true thieves." The choice of the feminine word for dog, *souka* [bitch], reflects the ongoing male chauvinistic attitude of the thieves.

THE PRETTY POLISH GIRL

Basia, a young Polish girl from Warsaw, had ended up in the Norilsk camp in August of 1946. In spite of having been subjected to two years of interrogation, she is still a seductive woman. A committee of NKVD judges (whom she never saw) sentenced her to twenty years of hard labor for "counter-revolutionary crimes." She is therefore working on a construction site, hauling bricks about on her back. She has to crawl up ladders and scaffolding to unload her load for the masons. The workdays are ten hours long.

One day the young architect Smirnov arrives at the site on an inspection visit. As he is climbing on the staging, trying to get to the first floor, he goes by a young woman prisoner loaded with bricks. The girl slips but Smirnov instinctively catches her and prevents her from falling. Fearing punishment, she apologizes profusely and Smirnov—still a novice—feels embarrassed and tries to reassure her, thus violating the regulations stating that employees cannot have any contact but professional ones with the inmates. They exchange a few words. Without thinking, Basia makes several observations on the management of the worksite. The architect is struck by the clarity and pertinence of her observations. This is because Basia is herself an architect with a diploma from the Polytechnic University of Warsaw. It's almost like Prince Charming and Cinderella right there in the middle of the Gulag! Smirnov is infatuated by this encounter and talks the head architect into reassigning Basia to the engineering department. This would be a real feat to have an inmate removed from the "general" worksite and transferred to a white-collar job. It is not by luck that the expression "extracted" is used for designating someone removed from hard labor assignments. The head architect knew of the University of Warsaw and decided to risk the request for the good of the project. However, it is the political commissar who is in charge... and, architect or not, the transfer of an inmate sentenced to hard labor for "counter-revolutionary crime" would be a total breach of regulation. The commissar was an old Tchekist and nostalgically believed firmly in Lenin's old dictum: "They should be assigned to the most painful and strenuous tasks." Ah! what a genius he was, that old Lenin! But, getting back to the young Polish girl, there was more bad news: upon closer inspection her dossier revealed several pernicious influences during her formative years in pre-war capitalist Poland. Worse yet, picking further into her past he—the commissar—discovers that Basia had participated in the Warsaw Uprising against the Nazis. They were on the western bank of the river in August 1944, while the Red Army held the eastern side and repeatedly refused to help the Polish insurgents desperately holding out opposite them. As a result, the Nazis had a free hand to massacre almost two hundred thousand civilians. Only after this debacle did the Red Army enter Warsaw in triumph to liberate the ruined city. Soon after, the NKVD launched a massive arrest of the survivors and Basia was amongst them. Inevitably, this Polish girl must hate the Soviets therefore she must be dangerous. She deserves to be punished. Of course, people like her would never give in. The Commissar would also remember the words of the great proletarian writer Gorky: "If the enemy doesn't surrender, crush him!"

In short, after two days in the engineering department, Basia was sent to a remote mine, pushing little wagons. She is not in high spirits then, one day, in the shaft where she was working, a filthy *zek* comes asking, "Where is the architect?" "It's me!" "Come quickly to the foreman's office, there's a telephone call for you, it's an emergency!"

Her friends push her to go. "Go ahead! We'll cover for you." With her heart beating out of her chest, Basia follows the messenger along the shafts. Her friends have high hopes.

Time goes by and still no sign of Basia. It is now time to go back to the barracks. She still hasn't returned. Searches are organized. Finally, they find her on the ground, unconscious, at the bottom of an abandoned well, her clothing in tatters, her neck and face covered with bruises and her naked thighs blotched with blood.

The good Soviet people call this "going under the tram," or "undergoing the *kolkhoz*," or "being put through the collective."

In 1956 Basia was released, long after Stalin's death. According to the official document, her charges were all fabricated.

TCHEREPANOV, THE WORKSITE BRIGADIER

Our team is hard at work. All of sudden comes the warehouse captain. I wonder what's brought him here today? He goes right over to the brigadier Tcherepanov. "Let's go!" "Where to?" the latter asks. "You'll see." Tcherepanov leaves us with several instructions and takes off with the warehouse captain.

After our workday we find him back in our barracks. He is somber, solemn. A crowd of *zeks* from the other barracks, equally solemn, surround him with much respect. "I am about to be released! They are going to let me go." A victim of the Great Purge like many other millions, Tcherepanov was sentenced "in due form" to ten years of hard labor for counter-revolutionary crimes he never committed.

For years thereafter, *zeks* told many details the story of how the warehouse captain came to get Tcherepanov to the worksite and took him to the local chief of the NKVD who even shook this poor *zek's* hand and said, "Well, well Comrade Tcherepanov [yes, he did say 'Comrade'], the party and the Soviet state have examined your dossier. They decided to proclaim you innocent and punish severely those who testified falsely against you. Both the party and the state are here to enforce justice!"

This took place during World War II. Once brought to the front, Tcherepanov soon paid the ultimate price on the field of honor "for the motherland and for Stalin." He never had time to kiss his wife and their four children goodbye, which in itself whould have been virtually impossible—being "members of the family of an enemy of the people" they were probably sent off to some remote part of Siberia. They might have heard about their husband and father's glorious death. Who knows. As of now, they are entitled to claim a pension.

THE TRUNK

There are six of us. We are escorted by two soldiers, one has a rifle with a fixed bayonet and the other holds a German shepherd on a leash who never stops barking. We are fortunate he doesn't bite. Our escorts look huge to us with their big fur hats, their sheepskin coats, and their sturdy felt boots. They ooze good health. Their cheeks are rosy, they are well fed. We envy them.

We make slow and difficult progress in the deep snow, striving to step in the imprints made by the one in front of us. Boris is leading. The soldiers make us cross the skin of ice on the Yenisei. At this point, the river is two kilometers wide and the ice is about two meters thick. We arrive, at last. We've marched four kilometres away from the compound. As we approach our destination, we can make out that it is an enormous tree trunk covered with snow. Boris gets a splinter of it out of the lining of his coat and examines it. "It's locust," he says, sadly. It is the heaviest wood. These logs are floated down here in the summer. The trunk is more than a meter across, and eight meters long, and probably weighs three or four tons.

Boris kicks away the snow in which it is buried and we can see that it's not really standing on the ground, but that it is deeply sunk in. During the warm season the bank was flooded, and as the water receded the tree trunk became buried in the muck. It has now become a chunk of ice as hard as rock. The thought of it depresses us, all the more so since we stopped walking and as a consequence the cold has become more penetrating.

After half an hour, the foreman arrives. He is a common law prisoner who is entitled to go around without an escort. This explains why he is late. He details our work assignment to Boris then proceeds to his 'office,' a tiny hut buried in the snow. "Send me a man to light the stove and watch the fire," he yells to Boris. We are all thinking, "Good Lord, let it be me!" Without hesitating, he designates Agapone, an eighty-year-old peasant. Agapone scrounges some kindling from underneath the snow, then leaves. There were six of us, down to five now.

Boris explains our tasks to us: with a metal bar and a pickaxe, we are supposed to extricate this enormous tree from its glacial armor so that a tractor can come and take it in tow. With that said, Boris goes into the "office" to write the "report" on our daily work. We all perfectly know how vital that document is because by playing with an array of data related to the complex and detailed "technical norms" and thanks to his influence and good relationships with the guards and brigadiers, Boris may provide us with some insufficient yet not catastrophic food rations. The report must be filled out on a standard form. However, since the authorities don't have one, you have to make do. Paper being scarce, even outside of the camps, almost anything can be used from shreds of papercrete to pieces of plywood, even birch bark. Now, we realize this is a delicate task, and that there are only four of us to confront this huge locust tree.

And that's not all: Crater-Face Valerka heads over to the "office" as the chimney starts to smoke. He is a thief, and the code of thieves forbid him to work. There is a saying, "A thief steals, everyone else works like a horse." We've all known this the hard way and for a long time. But why did Crater-Face Valerka ever accept to be escorted here? He probably thought he would be taken to the other worksite where we all worked yesterday. There he could have met up with his fellow hoods and done "a little business." The escorts never inform us of our destination, and only stick to the formula: "A step to the left or to the right is considered an escape attempt. The escort will fire without warning. Understood?"

It's only after several hours of dogged work that the three of us manage to remove the locust from the frozen ground. During that time, half of our labor force—i.e. the other three—stayed in the hut, with the foreman and the two escorts. Those two did get out once in a while to check on us. From inside, they couldn't see through the frosted panels.

A STUPID MISTAKE

This is serious. The senior warder just came into my cell without making a sound. The bolt didn't even squeak. The stooge who opened it for him stayed outside, keys in his hand, without closing the door, in accordance with the rules.

We are in 1948, in the pre-trial prison of the forced labor camp of Norilsk, above the Artic Circle. The "boarders" are convicts suspected of having committed a new crime, a new offence, although they are still serving out the time of their old sentence. They are common criminals, mostly thieves, recidivists and murderers. There are very few political prisoners like me, alone here in my cell for almost two years now. In the cells of the former ones, the guards are constantly busy between fights, arguments, and busted doors. My cell, on the contrary, must seem like a haven of tranquility!

The senior-warder scolds me like a disgruntled father with his mischievous son. "You're no thief! You're educated, so why would you make such a stupid mistake." His voice echoes in my cell like in a barrel and the guard standing outside my door only hears the last words. Another guard passing by asks, intrigued, "What's going on?" "Oh! He's made a stupid mistake," says my guard in a very assertive way. "Ah," answers the other one. You see, in the land of the Soviets, any information passed on by someone considered "competent" is considered to be the word of God.

As for the stupid mistake, well, this is what it was: with a tiny nail I tried to engrave on my aluminum bowl "Petri is a stoolie." This former inmate with whom I had spent many years behind the bars and barbed wire had turned out to be an informer to the police. Thanks to him I was sentenced, after a long fabricated trial, to twenty-five more years. This time, it was strictly enforced labor in a high security prison. Serving bowls would circulate amongst prisoners during the food distribution so the message I had attempted to scratch on mine was to warn my buddies down the line. Unfortunately, the senior-warden's paternal intervention spoiled my entire project...

THE BRAIN

Before his arrest in 1937, Alexander Fomitch had been the head of a department at the Ministry of Heavy Industries. He started as a simple steelworker and, thanks to his militant zeal, ended up in that prestigious position.

In spite of all those years of bureaucratic work he still hadn't forgotten his old skills, so that once he arrived in the camp, he managed to get himself assigned to the repair shop as a fitter, thus avoiding hard manual labor.

As he was a good worker, he was asked to train apprentices. Alexander Fomitch befriended one of them named Iourik, a twelve-year-old delinquent who reminded him of his grandson, Micha. He still had his entire life ahead of him. According to the local custom that has all children calling any adult "Uncle," Iourik called Fomitch 'Uncle Sacha.'

One day when they returned from one of their excursions on the worksites, Iourik erupted into the workshop all excited, "Uncle Sacha, I didn't know that brain was grey!" he blurted out, his eyes all lit up by this astonishing discovery. "Wild-Beast Grichka has just pounded Ivan's head in with a big metal bar! His head is whacked open and something splattered on the wall. It is all grey. I realized quickly that it was human brain. I have never seen that, a man's brain!"

THE CIGARETTE BUTT

Today he is carrying water in a big barrel attached to a horse-drawn wagon. When he arrives at the worksite, he discovers that it is a team of women working there. There are political and common law prisoners, young and old mixed. Some come to fetch water. The foreman, busy elsewhere, is not overseeing so our guy takes advantage of this opportunity to whisper into the ear of one of them that he often goes to the area reserved for the free personnel and that, thanks to his contacts, he has access to their store too.

"Is that true?" asks the astonished girl. "Yes, yes!" he assures her. She really needs a little package of tobacco and one kilo of bread, except that she is completely broke. "Anything can be arranged" he says pointing to a miserable hole not far off. She checks out the surroundings and heads off to the shack. It is pitch black inside, filthy, and reeking. The shack is used for a latrine. The girl stops facing the wall, pulls up her skirt, unbuttons her quilted leggings, lowers them just far enough and leans forward. Behind her, he undoes his fly as he pulls on his cigarette. The girl sees the reflection of the glow on the wall. "Let me finish your butt," she says, reaching for it from behind. The man takes a last drag on the cigarette and passes it to her while he penetrates her.

THE LIGHTBULB

He'd climbed up the pole and stolen the lightbulb. At any rate the clever system put in place to electrocute the potential thieves was out of order, or Chourik had known how to bypass it. Delighted with his success, he could already taste the bread. In exchange for the lightbulb he was to receive at least one kilo from the free workers on the worksite.

Bad luck though, he had been betrayed. A chauffeured car with two lieutenants from the local section of the State Security Bureau had come to take him to prison. Why two officers when just one simple corporal would have done as well? I don't know. I do know, however, that it could only be the organs of state security and by no means the local police: the pole in question was located in a zone controlled exclusively, and expressly, by the State Security Bureau. The next pole in the line, ten meters away, was controlled by the local police. But Chourik had chosen the first one.

His case being rather straightforward, and the accused making no denials, Chourik benefited from a legal instruction without physical abuse or excessive zeal on the part of the prosecutors, followed by a trial. As he was already fulfilling a sentence for robbery at the moment of the crime, he was sentenced as a recidivist to an additional three years. Six weeks went by between his arrest and his sentencing, and another two weeks before the formalities of his transfer to the labor camp, only fifteen minutes away by foot from the courthouse and the prison.

It took place in the boreal zone of Siberia in the early fifties. At that time, in the far-flung reaches of the empire, an officer of State Security and a commissar-interrogator each would be making about 3,500 rubles per month, or about 17 rubles an hour; a sergeant about 13. The daily cost of housing and feeding an inmate was about 9 rubles. If we add up all the expenses—transportation of the two security officers and the lieutenant (47 rubles) + an eight-week stay in prison for Chourik (551 rubles) + fifteen hours of work for the commissar (255 rubles), including lost wages for Chourik due to temporary lay-off (675 rubles)—this episode cost the Soviet state a total of 1,538 rubles.

At that time a lightbulb cost 78 rubles, but was impossible to find in the state's stores—the only existing legal retail stores.

THE SUPERIORITY OF LENINISM OVER TSARISM

During the First World War, a young Austrian lieutenant, Emerich Poglitsch, had been taken prisoner by the army of the tsar.

By 1947, he had become a councilman in Vienna—occupied at that time by the Russians—and once again found himself in a Russian prison.

It would be difficult to suspect Emerich of sympathies towards Marxism-Leninism. He was integrity personified. Yet, he had to admit that there was one point on which the Soviet camps could be said to have improved upon those of the old tsarist regime, and that was that you were no longer devoured by lice.

MAN IS NOT EQUAL TO A HORSE

You could see several dozen piles of tree trunks along the quay. About seventy yards from it there was a set of railroad tracks. In front of each pile was a team of *zeks* just shuffling around. They had to push the trunks one at a time over to the rail spur so that they could be quickly loaded onto the flatcars when the train arrived. To make things easier, they had laid out the trunks end to end in two lines like rails so that they could slide along. Weight varied according to the length, from four to eight meters, and their diameter, from twenty-five to forty centimeters and according to the species, either pine or locust, the heaviest of all the trees in Siberia. Usually there were four of us to roll the tree trunks along. The work was extremely strenuous, we were always bent over for ten hours straight.

Our fellow inmates to the right of us are rolling the trunks without a hitch, it seems. They are all veterans of the Gulag, peasants. On my left, the work is going along even better. Fritz-the-Gypsy (where on Earth did he get that name?) works alone with the draft horse that the camp administration gave him. He ties the horse to the stump of the trunk (much heavier than the top) and pushes the other end either with his left arm or his foot, holding the reins with the whip in his right hand.

We are all in deep admiration of his skill and the endless stream of curses that he throws at his unperturbed draft horse. Compared to him we are all useless! We, that is to say: Epifanov, a professor of Marxism-Leninism who taught at the Academy of Mines in Moscow until 1937, the year of the Great Purge; Ivanov, a colonel in the Red Army, who was chief of the general staff; Professor Kozyrev—the director of research at the Leningrad Observatory, and your servant, a former secret agent for the Comintern...

After ten hours of work, as we were waiting for the escort to take us back to the camp, Professor Kozyrev turns to me and says, "What an imperfect creature man is! To think that after millions of years of natural selection, these four specimens of human beings are still inferior to a poor draft horse..."

THE CYCLOPS

We are rolling trunks over to the railroad tracks. There are thousands of them, tens of thousands, piled up three or four meters high. Their lengths vary, at one end they are all fairly even but, at the other, some of them stick out here and there. It is winter, and when one is suddenly taken with nature's call—to avoid freezing your buttocks in some snow bank, and before you pull down your pants—you just perch yourself on one of the trunks that stick out of the pile.

One fine day, somebody notices that Ivan has gone missing. It couldn't be an escape attempt. We are in the Arctic, where would he go? He might have left looking for something to eat. *Zeks* are always on the lookout for that.

The brigadier is aware that Ivan and I are friends. He sends me out to look for him. It's already dark, and here I am meandering amongst the fallen trees. Suddenly, I see an enormously bloated, pale face right in front of me and, in the middle, there is one eye just staring at me, motionless. I feel a shiver down my spine but I approach all the same, until I realize it is somebody's ass. It is my friend Ivan's! Holy shit! Comfortably wedged in between two of the higher tree trunks, he'd just fallen asleep. That happens to us sometimes when we stop moving. We may fall asleep crumpled up into any old position. There are even inmates who can sleep while walking. Except that in his case, he is running the risk of freezing not only his buttocks but also certain other very delicate parts of his anatomy. By waking him up—which wasn't an easy task—I probably saved him from an amputation...

THE ROTTEN FISH

We're in December 1941, in Dodinka, the port of the forced labor camp of Norilsk. We're hitched to our task: extracting planks from the ice. These planks come from sawmills several hundred kilometers up-river. They have been here since the summer. They are all attached together in giant blocks of four meters wide by four meters long, at least, and maybe two to three meters high. When they arrived several months ago, they were pushed as close to the bank as possible, so that when the water receded they could be reached. As the *zeks* were assigned to other more pressing projects during the summer, the blocks of planks just sat there. In the meantime they have buried themselves in the muck. At this very moment they are held in solid ice covered with a thick blanket of snow.

We begin by removing the thick layer of hard packed snow. Then using metal bars as levers we extract the planks one by one from their icy shell. It is a very harsh and difficult job. The planks are each forty centimeters wide, five centimeters thick and more than four meters long.

We've been working for hours, and our pile is already half gone when a horrible stench grabs us all by the throat. A putrid stench of rot—and it's −30oC!

In a minuscule space between two planks, buried deep within the enormous block of wood, there was a little puddle of water left unfrozen by the insulating thickness of the wood. In that little puddle was the carcass of a tiny little fish, not even four centimeters long. That was the cause of the stench! Without thinking twice, Aliocha—with whom I've been hauling the planks—leaps on it like a hawk, grabs it and swallows it immediately. He's a peasant and he comes from a *kolkhoz*. He knows what hunger is—from long before the Gulag. He was only twelve years old when his village was collectivized.

SHAME

He was wearing a full-length soft leather coat, and looked the part of a gentleman when he arrived in our cell at Moscow's Butyrka Prison in 1937. He didn't even look particularly surprised by this sudden string of unfortunate circumstances. Inevitably, as an old Bolshevik, he must have known a lot about the regulations and customs of Lenin and Stalin's Party.

Latsis was a proletarian from Riga and a Bolshevik from the very outset of bolshevism. As early as 1917, he had taken part in the attack on the Winter Palace in Petrograd. Forever faithful to the party, he had enjoyed a meteoric career. By the beginning of the thirties he had become the director of a department of the National Soviet Petrol Company.

I lost track of him as a result of a prisoner transfer from within the prison. These systematic prisoner transfers are intended to prohibit inmates from making friends. The Soviet authorities always viewed these as embryonic elements of "anti-revolutionary groups" with no other goal than the "overthrow of the Soviet state."

Thus, in much the same manner two years later in 1939, I ran into Latsis again. Once our respective "investigations" were completed, we were sentenced in absentia by a simple decision the infamous Osso (1), a special board, an administrative court of the state security organs, and then we found ourselves in the same convoy headed to an unknown destination.

When—after several weeks of transit—we arrived, we were separated. However, as Evgenia Guinzbourg described it so accurately in her book *Into the Whirlwind*, transporting inmates across the biggest nation on earth is a long and arduous adventure that occasionally allows strong, lasting friendships to emerge amongst its "travelers." So, when I ran into Latsis six years later, it was like being with a close family member.

This time, we were beyond the Arctic Circle in the second compound section of the Norilsk camp, which encompassed about twenty more camps spread out over an area bigger than the size of France. My sentence—like that of my friend—was nearing its end. Unfortunately, as we both knew that in the large majority of cases once the term was up the inmates were notified they would be *kept in confinement until further notice based on USSR NKVD Instruction No. 224.* This regulation also applied to certain types of non-political prisoners, especially those who had been convicted of banditry. From what we could tell, this decree was issued by the commissar of State Security. In any case one thing was certain: it was enforced for the first time on June 23rd, 1941—the day after the Nazi attack against the USSR. Strangely enough, certain political prisoners who were victims of it but continued to proclaim their belief in the regime would nonetheless strive to justify this scandalous and illegal measure. "Now that we are at war with the worst enemy humankind has ever known," they would say, "it is completely normal that the government should do everything that it thinks necessary to protect itself against a fifth column." "But you there, speaking to me, you are not an enemy of the Soviet People?" "Of course not! The only thing is that the government is not aware of that!"

One day I, like so many others, was notified that I was *to be detained until further notice* based on Instruction No 224. I asked to be shown this document. The security officer of the compound was surprised by this request. Out of the two or three thousand *zeks* under his supervision, whose great majority was affected by the decree, not one had expressed the desire to see the printed words. For the inmates as well as the authorities, it was merely an established fact. "How strange that you want to see the decree!" the officer said. "Even me, I've never had it in my hands. Furthermore, I wouldn't let you go without having received a specific order. I don't see what the problem is." He actually looked a bit amused. Even Latsis, my friend, seemed surprised by my attitude.

At the end of two years, without any explanation, I was finally released. Actually, you could say, I was assigned a residence on the other side of the barbed wire. The only official identification I had was a sheet of paper that had to be stamped every two weeks by the local police. On the sheet was a warning: *If more than fifteen days have elapsed since the last stamp, this receipt is no longer valid. The carrier will be considered a fugitive and liable for legal pursuit.* A mere smattering of liberty, but it was at least that. As for Latsis, he was still waiting his turn to be released. I was ashamed. Why me and not him? Go figure!

One year later, completely arbitrarily, my friend was liberated. But he received a proper identity card with which he was free to go back home to Moscow, seven thousand miles away. As for me, I was arrested again several months later and, this time, I was sentenced to twenty-five years.

I had no reason to be ashamed anymore.

NOTES

(1) *Ossoboïe Sovechtchanié* : OGPU special board entitled to administer in absentia extra-judicial sentences of varying decrees of severity, including death by shooting. This board dates back to Lenin (see *troika* p. 51)

Almost half of the jailed population of the USSR in the 1940-50s was condemned by OSSO. Being extra-judicial, special board decisions were final so that individuals sentenced unjustly could not file an appeal. The institution was abolished in September 1953.

THE MACHINE TO READ ONE'S MIND

A scratchy voice was quietly humming a tune. It was very monotonous. It was always the same tune, for hours at a time. It's Anatoli Pavlovitch, the accountant. Bent over his large accounts book, he fills in columns and columns of figures very patiently. He would dunk his fountain pen into an inkwell of the same old purple ink, and hum and hum without pausing. Every once in a while, he would put down his pen and crank the handle of the arithmometer, the first digital mechanical calculator. Then he might stop humming. You could hear the noise of the handle snapping back. Anatoli Pavlovitch would glance at the result of the operation and pick up the fountain pen with his tobacco-stained fingers to note down the figure shown on the machine. Then the humming would resume once more. I'll go insane, I thought. How can I put an end to this torture? I tried to reason with myself. How can I call this 'torture?' Here I am, comfortably seated in an office, keeping warm, all clean, holding a fountain pen, whereas yesterday I was hauling coal from morning to night, freezing to death, sweating, every pore full of fine, microscopic coal dust. This I owe to Volodia, the brigadier in charge of handling the material. Several years ago we were in the same convoy that departed from Moscow in trains to the transit camp of Krasnoiarsk, then in the hold of a barge as far as Doudinka, above the Arctic Circle. Seven thousand kilometers in three months. This kind of trial often bonds those who endure them together. Volodia recognized me among the dockers who unloaded the coal barges. He found me a spot on the worksite office. What a stroke of luck! It is the end of August, winter is beginning. My job is to prepare some old documents the forms Soviet bureaucracy is so fond of yet keeps running out of.

But how can I put a stop to this aggravating humming? I find a way. Before being sentenced for malpractice and sent to the Gulag, Anatoli Pavlovitch had been employed in one of the state trading posts in the Arctic where the indigenous hunters had to sell their furs to the Russians at prices set by the state. He was well acquainted with the region, as well as the customs of the people. To make him talk, and therefore stop his unbearable humming, I would constantly quizz him on this topic—I cannot think of any other. He would answer with good humor, except that when he had nothing left to add he would resume his humming. And I would again storm him with other questions, always on the same topic, totally lacking imagination.

If I don't just come out and ask him to stop humming, it is for two reasons: first, Anatoli Pavlovitch is sixty years old and I am just thirty. It would seem impolite for me to make any comment about it—this is one of the vestiges of my pre-Gulag education which hasn't yet been erased; second, I have learned that one should never reveal any weakness to one's enemy because he might find a way to turn it into his advantage; furthermore, in this ruthless world, everyone is your enemy, real or potential. This is one of the many lessons of the Gulag.

Winter goes by, and at the beginning of May I am being transferred by order of the director to a barracks "of intensified regime" with no explanation. "Intensified regime" means that you are assigned the hardest manual labor, and after work are locked up in the barracks with bars on the windows, padlocks on the doors, and a latrine bucket inside while the other inmates are free to get around inside the compound unit.

In mid-September winter returns. The blanket of snow that covers the tundra becomes thicker and thicker, the wind more and more glacial and penetrating. I have finally been released from the "intensified regime," again without any explanation. Only the director could shine any light on this enigma, so I requested an interview, which was granted, and even more surprising is that he explained it all to me: "We have been told that you were planning an escape. Your abiding interest for the indigenous people was the reason for suspicion, that's why we made sure you'd spend that pleasant part of the year in a safe area." "But escape is virtually impossible from here!" I exclaimed surprised. "We know that, but the spring is when all escapes take place." "But I never had any intention of escaping!" "I have no way of knowing what is going on in your head. The machine to read your mind has yet to be invented." For a brief second, I almost wish it had. Then, maybe thousands of innocent victims who never harbored any ill thoughts towards the Soviet regime would have been spared.

As for Anatoli Pavlovitch I don't hold a grudge against him. Here any citizen who doesn't report even the least suspicious behaviour is automatically an accomplice. Anatoli Pavlovitch was well aware of it. In his mind my unusual interest for those "ignorant" people of the Arctic was a clear indication that I intended to escape.

Except that I was never interrogated personally about this, and quite rightly, so is it possible anymore to prove a lack of intention?

THE HEAP OF GARBAGE

There are brigades of inmates that manage to fulfill the *output norms* and even exceed them, thus managing to receive 100 percent of the food ration, perhaps even more. How is that possible? It is either because those brigades are composed of former peasants who are used to hard manual labor and whom the Gulag has not yet broken, or because the brigadier knows how to cheat, and make use of the infamous *tufta*, finding a way to juggle all the complexities of state production norms; or else he has found a way to corrupt the foreman, the work assigner, and the camp administrator as well as the innumerable representatives of the employer who have to countersign his *voucher on work completed* before it is handed to the *norm setter* whose calculations will set the food rations.

In short, it happens that there are *zeks* who are not starving, and who actually throw away what's left of their food, like heads of herrings, for example. This, naturally, attracts the garbage pickers who are far more numerous than those who throw out the fish heads.

It is not only physical hunger that drives a man to pick through the garbage, but also—for those who have profound experience of deprivation—the haunting spectre of remembered starvation.

There are two types of garbage pickers: those who come equipped with an old rusty can with some water in it to rinse their food before they eat it—because people always piss on the trash pile—and the others who omit this ritual, like that old European scholar, author of several philosophy books, whom I can still see today.

No one can say that he will never become a garbage picker.

THE PRICE OF A MOUTHFUL OF BREAD

"Where did you get that bread?" Frantic, his eyes as round and wide as fish eyes, the wretched soul hurries to swallow what he has in his mouth. He is squeezing in his hand the remains of a sticky and compact ration of rye bread while an iron hand grabs him by his neck and shakes him vigorously. They just hauled him from his hiding spot under the lower bunk, thus putting him on display for the entire barracks to see.

Emaciated, dirty, in tattered rags, the poor wretch has no idea what's in store for him. The only thing that matters now is the sublime taste of that heavy and glutinous bread in his mouth and then in his stomach : the sweet bulge gently expanding within the walls of his belly, thereby forestalling, if only for a moment, the gnawing torture of hunger.

He was still chewing when the first blows rained down on him. Awkward, uncoordinated, hesitant punches. Everyone knows the law: stealing the bread ration of a prisoner leads to a collective beating. The saying clearly states it, "He who steals the bread ration earned by bloody sweat will be beaten to death." You can steal everything else—clothes, shoes, soup, sugar, packages—but the sacred bread ration, the staple food of a *zek*. The old-timers say that in the old days no thief would ever have stolen a bread ration, not even from a pigeon. Unfortunately things have changed since then, even in the thief's world.

Surrounded by a tight circle of onlookers, the bread stealer is beaten violently and hatefully. Those who cannot get close to him stretch out their arms to punch him from over the heads of the others. His groans—though at first like moans—become harrowing. The man is on the ground; they are kicking him and beating him all over his body. It goes on and on. Then the cries stop. You can only hear the heavy thuds accompanied by "Agh, Agh!" for a long time. Little by little the crowd disperses. Motionless, formless, the cadaver lies on the floor. In the trickle of blood that spills out of his mouth you can see a small half-chewed chunk of bread.

THE SPARROW ON THE WINDOWSILL

It is December 1950, in the KGB prison of Krasnoiarsk, deep in Siberia. A sparrow just perched on the "louver" of my cell window. In prison slang, the "louver" is the opaque shield made out of wood or metal and mounted—seldomly in frosted glass—outside a cell window to prevent the "tenant" from looking outside. It is usually installed in such a way that all that can be seen from the cell is a thin band of sky at the very top of the window. It would have been possible to see more by sticking one's cheek against the wall, right under the window. But the regulations are specific, it is strictly forbidden to get near it. For failure to obey... the cooler.

Thus observing the correct distance, I admire the sweet and fresh little bird that is thumbing its nose in broad daylight at the all-powerful KGB who has kept me prisoner now in its camps and prisons for thirteen years without ever convicting me in due process, and who has just informed me—still without a trial—that I received an extension of sentence of twenty-five years.

As carefree as cheeky, the little sparrow hops around, chirps, just preening and smoothing its feathers. It is because its feathers are all covered with soot. It is winter in Siberia and the little bird is obliged to spend the nights in the chimney. This happens a lot here.

I watch this little foolhardy bird for a long time, and when the jailer peeks in at me through the Judas hole, I pretend to be looking at something else.

Finally, my little visitor lifts his tail, relieves himself, and flies away. He lifted my spirits and it lasted quite a while.

VOLODIA BOOK, HE NEVER STEALS

Volodia Book is here because of his Dutch background. Peter the Great brought one of his ancestors here from Russia to work in the naval shipyards. It certainly was a steep price for his descendant to pay. The NKVD, ever vigilant, doesn't make mistakes. They knew how to "unmask" this Dutch spy.

Even though he is given the same rags to dress in as the rest of us, he still knows how to wear them almost elegantly. In spite of the filth in the barracks and the dirt at the worksites, he is always as clean as possible and most courteous. When he speaks to someone, he looks them straight in the eyes, whether is it the head of the camp or the filthiest of our "goners." As famished as the rest of us, he doesn't inhale his meager ration the way we do. He eats calmly, dare I say, with much dignity.

But what is most extraordinary is that he never steals. Ever. Though stealing, especially food, is considered almost normal in a forced labor camp since we are all subjected by the regime to an implacable famine. It is already enough to consider that, theoretically, it is "forbidden" to steal the sacred bread ration of another inmate. That's the only thing forbidden, as for the rest... It is assumed that the famished convicts have the moral right to help themselves to whatever they see whenever it is available, especially when it is public goods. For example, someone may "trip" while unloading boxes of pasta. The box falls and breaks open. In the blink of an eye the alerted buddies fill up their pockets. We'll cook them later in the barracks after work if we succeed in smuggling them undetected. Or else, when carrying bags of flour, someone makes a hole in the fabric and fills up an empty can. Later, we'll mix that with some water, and roll the dough into balls we will swallow raw, or maybe we'll even allow ourselves the luxury to cook them. Of course, there are frequent searches, and it is not easy to get away with tricks like these, but you don't want to miss out on such an opportunity! However, Volodia always refuses to participate in these thefts. This might make him more suspicious to us, but we know him well enough and trust him.

Eight years later, after I had long since lost track of Volodia, I happened to meet a prisoner during another transfer who gave me news of him. I learned that he was well and still his old self. Obviously, the Soviet system had had no effect on him. That is extremely rare, as the Gulag teaches its inmates that "it is not the work but the scams that nourish you," and that "no one survives without cheating and stealing."

The Gulag had not succeeded in "rehabilitating" Volodia Book.

A GOOD GUY

He rolls his cigarette in a scrap of old newspaper, and grabs a coal from the fire to light it. His hands are enormous and very calloused, he doesn't even feel the scorch from the fire. Stepan Loukitch sucks hard on his cigarette. There is no foreman, no brigadier, no one to watch over us and the escort guards are not at our heels. We make ourselves comfortable on some tree trunks, near the fire. The construction work to which we have been assigned will have to wait.

Stepan Loukitch remembers the days when he was a longshoreman in Saratov, on the Volga. As always, his wife Macha figures in his tales. She is a little on the simple side that Macha, but what devotion! She was not in favor of Stepane's affiliation to the Communist Party but she made no reproach. She said nothing when he was made President of the Association of Atheist Supporters. It was because of these activities that he was later appointed Head of National Education in the area. He was done with the filthy dirty mule work of a proletarian!

Unfortunately, there was the horrible year of 1937, the year of the Great Purge. At the end of a fabricated trial, Stepan was sentenced to fifteen years of forced labor and was swallowed by the Gulag, like millions of others.

His family was immediately expelled from their beautiful apartment. Macha, who had no occupational training, was forced to work as a cleaner. She also had to hide the fact that she was the wife of an "enemy of the people." Their two children were excluded from the Communist Youth League, and therefore denied entrance to university.

When I first met Stepan in 1939 in the transit prison of Viatka, he was a broken man. I went for many years afterwards without running into him again until, in 1952, during another transfer, I meet him inadvertently in the Central Prison of Aleksandrovsk, near Lake Baikal. He looked good. His beloved Macha would regularly send him packages to improve his meager prisoner's rations. His sentence was about to end and he was soon to be freed. He was already making plans. "As with all political prisoners, I won't be allowed to go home and will be under house arrest somewhere in a remote part of eastern Siberia. I will, however, be free and I'll make a good living. I'll be eating better so that inevitably there will be the remaining problem of my sex life. Well, I guess I'll take a wife. I am fifty-eight. This is my last chance." "You are going to be unfaithful to Macha?" "Not at all. I am going to write her and tell her not to wait for nothing. I am a good guy, ain't I?"

SHARED HAPPINESS

Colonel Armster had been incarcerated in the Moabit Prison in Berlin, as a result of the assassination attempt against Hitler on 20 July 1944. The generals—against whom overwhelming proof—was presented had already been executed. Colonel Armster, along with a few others, had escaped the death penalty due to lack of evidence, which explains why they were all still alive when the Red Army liberated Berlin in May 1945.

I don't know what happened after that. But here I am in our cell of the prison of Aleksandrovsk in Western Siberia in June 1955, waiting in line behind Colonel Armster, for the watery noontime soup to be poured out. Like the rest of us, Colonel Armster is thin, shorn, and dressed in the same striped pyjamas. There are about thirty of us in the line, in front of a door that remains closed. Only the food hatch is open. Its flap opens only from the outside of the cell and folds down and outwards, forming a small ledge on which the bowl is placed. The serving girl in the hallway holds it with her left hand, protected by a glove of doubtful cleanliness, and after having vigorously stirred the content of her bucket with the ladle in her right hand, pours some into the bowl and replaces it on the ledge. The receiver then takes it religiously in his hands at the risk of burning himself because the bowls are made of aluminum, and solemnly walks away.

The serving girl is over thirty. She is not particularly pretty, and doesn't wear any make-up. She does her work, that's all. We are all very thankful to her because she goes to the trouble of stirring the bottom of the container. The soup is very watery and any possible solids—fishbones if it's fish soup, ends of nerves and ligaments if it's meat soup—would stay in the bottom. Our server is a corporal of the guard with the NKVD but she never appears in her uniform. She is always dressed as a simple Russian peasant girl. Her superiors tolerate this infringement to regulations. We call her affectionately

"Macha" amongst ourselves. Her gestures are precise and quick. The line at the window moves quickly. Soon it's Colonel Armster's turn. He hands his bowl over to Macha, leans down and says very politely, "*Kartoffel!*" For the eleven years he has been imprisoned in the Soviet prisons, he still hasn't learned the language of Pushkin and Lenin. It so happens that in Russian the word for potato is also *kartoffel*. Over the Colonel's shoulder I can see Macha's blushing smile. She mimes a gesture of helplessness, as if to offer excuses—Internal Regulations prohibit conversations between the prison staff and the prisoners, except when giving orders.

Before walking away with his bowl, the Colonel turns around with a radiant and almost triumphant look, "If she had had some, she would have given me some!" I am touched that he would share his happiness with me.

AH! GIRLS, GIRLS!

Our freightcar has left the Central Prison of Aleksandrovka, near Lake Baikal, bound for an unknown destination, as usual. Here we are in transit at the prison of Irkutsk. There are twenty of us in a cell: some Austrians; a German; a very old merchant from Mukden; a professor of economics and general for the Kuomingtang named Wang Tsie-Fou; several prisoners— half of them political, half delinquents, one of whom is a recidivist who has spent almost his whole life in prison; and, finally, the young son of a Ukrainian patriot.

It is February 1956, three years after the death of Stalin. The Austrians and the Germans are convinced that they are being transferred west to be handed to the Allies. The merchant from Mukden, imposing in his long Chinese robe, remains silent. As for Wang Tsie-Fou, his friend, he swears that justice will triumph in the end and conquer the Bolsheviks, but he doesn't know how or when. The young Ukrainian is convinced that the Ukrainian issue is the key to the world's problems and that soon Ukraine will regain her independence. The semi-political prisoners and delinquents don't believe in anyone or anything.

However, there is one thing that interests everyone here—except for the merchant from Mudken—that is, that there are female prisoners in the next cell. They are all delinquents. We are able to communicate with them through the window. The recidivist sings sentimental old romantic songs to them in a low voice. They express their joy by tapping on the wall.

In transit prisons like this one, there is a certain carelessness. Graffiti and writing on the walls often remain a long time before they are erased. The Kuomintang general, a veteran of the Russian prisons, grabs my attention to look at an obscene drawing of a naked woman with her legs spread wide.

We install phone links—wireless—with the women's cell. It is most simple: to speak you just put the bottom of your drinking cup on the wall with your mouth on the opening. On the other side, to listen to the speaker, you do the opposite and put the opening against the wall and stick your ear on the bottom of your cup. It is not exactly stereophonic but we manage to hear each other. The guard in the hallway doesn't hear a thing, even more so considering that here, unlike the the usual quiet of prisons (internal regulations prohibit "disruption of prison silence"), there is constant noise from comings and goings in the hallways.

Eventually some closer relationships are established from both sides of the wall. The Austrians in our cell receive some packages from abroad and the exotic edibles that are passed to our neighbours may have borne fruit. Each one finds a partner. One day, one of the girls tells her partner she has succeeded in removing one of the metal feet of her bed. She decides to start digging a hole in the wall. Clearly the object is not suited for that type of work, more so since the building, which was constructed perhaps at the beginning of the century is quite solid. Nevertheless, by taking shifts and thanks to the surrounding noise, the girls are able to work for hours on end. Finally, after several days' work, the foot of the bed pierces the wall. For their part, the boys on my side get busy and work at enlarging the hole. We can already shake hands... Things are moving right along and soon we'll be able to walk from one cell to another. Our achievement goes unnoticed by the guards who come by and count us twice daily. For them to see the hole they would have to look under the lower berth.

The atmosphere becomes more and more charged and only the merchant of Mukden remains unimpressed and, seemingly, unconcerned. He looks like a statue. When I start talking to him in an excuse to practice my rusty Chinese, he makes no allusion whatsoever to the project going on right in our cell, as though he never even noticed. In his world, just like in the Gulag, there are three sacrosanct rules: "see nothing, say nothing, hear nothing." The Japanese use three monkeys to symbolize this: one covers his eyes with his hands, another covers his mouth, and the third covers his ears. I can still re-member the little ivory statue we had on our Louis XV style console in our sitting-room. I was fascinated by it as a child. In the Soviet Union, the least insignificant word can be turned into a mortal trap.

Professor Wang Tsie-Fou, on the other hand, is getting more and more excited. He has been imprisoned for ten years during which he hasn't had many chances to encounter women and, from what we can tell, he seems to care a lot. Nonetheless, he is worried that the authorities may discover the scheme, and fears the aftermath.

We are closely following the whole operation. Even those who do not participate in the digging and "see nothing," know exactly how things stand: the hole has grown bigger, we can touch hands and we can see faces. Once the daily work is done, the diggers wash their hands carefully so as not to attract the jailer's attention. One day the hole has become so big that the next day we will certainly be able to truly "make contact" with our sisters! Alas! That very night, after the lights-out signal, an officer came into our cell followed by two guards. They proceeded to go right toward the hole, told us to gather our belongings and dispatched us into different cells.

There you go! At the last minute, everything shot to hell! Luckily we aren't sent to the cooler, and the instructions for our next trans-fer have arrived.

ANOTHER PLANET

We are brought back to our barracks after a ten or twelve hour work-day. We swallow our dishwater that the Gulag calls 'soup' and, com-pletely exhausted, crash onto the planks of our berths. Squashed one against the other like herrings in their cans, we immediately fall asleep.

Ceaseless Moscow propaganda spewing endlessly from loudspeak-ers permeates the barracks. The TASS News Agency sanitizes the foreign news: in some country the police have dispersed a peaceful demontration of workers using massive brutality; in another a flood has carried away entire villages, causing hundreds of poor peasants to die; elsewhere a capitalist justice system has condemned some inno-cent workers to be sentenced to three, sometimes four years of prison.

In the barracks, those who aren't yet asleep listen without even trying to compare their situation with the ones they hear about. There are over one hundred and fifty inmates in this cell and not one of them has received less than a ten-year sentence of forced labor, based on fabricated evidence and, on top of that, we have all been judged not by a court but pursuant to a specific administrative code. Those victims of "class justice," along with the TV presenter speak-ing from Moscow, are nothing if not out of this world.

It is 1940. Twelve years earlier as a young Communist activist in Pilsudski's capitalistic Poland, I was brought before the court to answer charges about my underground activities. Contradictory de-bates, lawyers, pleadings, witnesses for the prosecution, forty kilos of illegal flyers used for incriminating evidence led to a sentence of nine months in prison. Did that really happen? Today, confined in the Gulag barracks, I cannot believe it. It seems like another world.

Sixteen years have gone by. It is now 1956, at the very beginning of the timid de-stanilisation undertaken by Krutschev. I am standing here in front of the French Embassy in Moscow. Two burly Soviet policemen stand in my way. Politely one of them asks, "Where are you going?"

"To my country's embassy."

"Your papers, please." I show him the letter I received from the Consul Général, in both French and Russian. A note for the Soviet authorities requests that they assist the bearer, a French citizen, in his request to return home. "Very well," says the policeman, "My comrade is going to call the ambassador to check if he will see you now." Always polite, he gently pushes me over to the side alley where no one can see you. While the other policeman "contacts the ambassador," he watches me. It's taking forever. Maybe he can't find a phone booth. My guard has left his post for a moment, I quickly climb up the fence and fall over onto the other side in the snow. I am now in French territory! The first time in twenty years... and what years they have been!

I sprint towards the main building of the embassy, open a door and here I am—transported into another world, onto another planet. A beautifully furnished room with a nicely waxed floor, a beautiful oriental rug, some green plants, a low table stacked with French magazines and newspapers—the first I have seen in twenty years! Such luxurious and fine quality print! Here is *Le Temps*, actually no, the familiar print spells something different, it's *Le Monde*.

"Sir, you are going to tread snow all over my newly waxed floors!" says an elegant woman holding a watering can in one hand. Dumbfounded by my unanticipated intrusion, she regains her composure only gradually. I hear my own language spoken by a native French woman. Such intoxicating music, what emotion. For this charming diplomat's wife I was an extraterrestrial coming straight from another planet... (1)

NOTES
(1) Soviet realities being as they were, it is only years later that I was able to return to France.

123

TWENTY YEARS LATER

It has been quite a while since I was freed. I am walking around Warsaw. It's Sunday, the weather is fine, and I am walking near an outdoor market. It is a crowded street. Two men pass me. One of them holds against his chest an already-open carton of cigarettes which he almost drops on the ground. There is something strange about the appearance of these men. I examine them more carefully. They have dark skin, black hair, and they are a bit tipsy. The man with the carton catches my eye and asks me, waving a 500 zloty bill in my face, "Could you give me change for a 500 zloty bill?" Wow, that guy has a strange accent. I wonder where he is from. I take out my pocketbook and start to count my one-hundred-zloty notes. We are all walking abreast and he shows me the pack of cigarettes. "You want one?,"

"No, thanks. I don't smoke."

"Well, then you must be quite a drinker. Your hands are shaking."

"Nope, I don't drink. If my hands tremble like that it is because I spent too much time in prison." The man perks up. "Which one?" "Butyrka." "Me, it was Taganka."(1) I hand him five one-hundred-zloty bills. "Here you are." "No, thank you. You only have one-hundred-zloty notes. We need smaller change than that." With that said, they go away. Evidently, they tried to pass a counterfeit bill to me but decided against it in the end.

What a strange story. Two strangers meet in a city in a country foreign to both of them and they introduce themselves by mentioning their respective Moscow prison, at which point one abandons his attempt to scam the other.

No doubt about it, solidarity exists! Gulagians of the world…

NOTES
(1) Moscow prison, not to be mistaken with the famous playhouse!

THE JAPANESE

"Halt!" I obey. I find myself next to a door, down a long hallway. It is grey like all the others. The number 48 is written on it in black. The *corridor man* (turnkey) approaches my escort showing no interest whatsoever in my humble self. He takes a quick glance at the form shoved under his nose, then opens the two huge padlocks one after the other, puts his big key in the door lock, turns it twice, opens the door, shows me in and immediately closes it behind me.

In front of me, opens a big cell. Behind me, the noise of the two padlocks being replaced and the squeaking of the key in the door lock. Then, just silence. Thirty faces are all turned towards me. They are Asians. Most are seated cross-legged on their beds, all dressed in flimsy striped pyjamas, the same ones that I was issued upon my arrival in this insitution two weeks ago. All these men are very skinny. It appears that they are all subsisting solely on the rations given to them by the prison, without any additional ones. It has been that way for a long time. I know; I am in the same boat.

Only here, I am totally amazed by something unusual and disarming: the dignity in their stares. In those eyes there is no trace of that starving-jackal-like vacancy that so dominates the Gulag. That is the first impression I have of the Japanese.

This was in 1949, in the Central Prison of Aleksandrovka. At the time I had already been in the Gulag for twelve years. Twelve years of sticky rancid filth— full of lies, perfidy, disillusionment, humiliation, provocations, arrogance, perversion, hypocrisy, starvation, cold, and terror. Those challenges were all the more painful for me because they were inflicted by "pure and authentic" Russian Communists, the same ones who carried the torch of Marxism-Leninism to the four corners of the world. Me—as a young French Communist—I was more than proud to participate in this glorious task. In my enthusiasm I was more than happy to pay the price. Alas, that price was not paid to the "enemy" but to the "friend."

There in that cell with former officers of the Japanese Imperial Army, for the first time in so many years, I had the impression that I was breathing fresh air. I was astonished later when I learned that by locking me up with "Oriental monkeys" the Commissar intended to humiliate and punish me. I must say that I certainly didn't tell him otherwise.

Later on, from 1949 to 1956, because of the accidental encounters that occured during transfers, I frequently found myself locked up with Japanese. Their civil demeanor, discipline, and cleanliness was such a contrast to this sordid world that each of these meetings was like a blast of fresh air for me, a calm and serene sunrise. For reasons that I never understood, the Soviet authorities had decided not to mix the Japanese officers with the Gulag prisoners. Maybe therein lies one of the reasons why they managed to keep their integrity and their culture, those values that the Gulag sought to destroy.

Most of my Japanese cellmates only spoke their native language, which I didn't know. However, I fondly remember the conversations I had in English with Prince Konoe Fumitaka, son of the former prime minister. It was there that I met Misao, the future Professor Gosuke Uchimura. We would speak either in English, Russian, or Chinese.

In 1952 or 1953 the Soviet authorities thought that, if they treated their Japanese prisoners more humanely, they might be able to gain some political advantages from them. They were, as a result, allowed to correspond with their families back in Japan for the first time in seven or eight years. Misao generously shared the warmth found in the letters from his wife Hamako with me. He had had no news from the outside world for more than fifteen years. Little by little, in the brief messages so severely censured, Hamako managed to slip in, "Say hello to your friend for me." Each time she did it, it felt as though I had been caressed through the thick walls of my prison by a puff of fresh air from the free world. I am ever grateful to them. Ever since, Misao and his family have remained my friends. For Manami, Rurika and their children, I am "Uncle Jacques."

Strangely enough, during my entire stay in the Gulag, it was amongst the Japanese that I felt the closest to France and her culture from which I had by then been separated by at least twelve thousand kilometers and,—more than anything—by twelve years in the Gulag.

SON!

Moscow, 1937. Stalinist terror is in full swing. We are more than eighty inmates in a cell designed for twenty five. It is August. We are suffocating. Not a single drop of water is left in our big kettle. The water is distributed at set times and we've already had it. The wise men of the cell ponder on this major issue: how to ask for water without letting this request be interpreted as a sign of discontent and more so of collective discontent, something most serious. Secondly, how to address the issue to a simple second-class jailer who nevertheless represents the Soviet power and therefore Stalin? It must be noted that our wisemen were all big shots in the Party and pillars of the regime until the day of their arrest. Astounded by their comprehension-defying adventure, they still make objections and reaffirm their unrequited faithfulness to Leninism-Stalinism. They persist in thinking there has been a major mistake that will soon be corrected, and that they will soon return to their original positions. Amongst them is a former director of the Central Committee Department, a CEO of some coalmine company, a former armored division general, a former professor of Marxism-Leninism from Party University, and so on.

An old worker with grey hair, the only working class one in our cell, gets out from the berth below. It is where, from lack of space, half of the inmates sleep. He heads out to the latrine bucket and, while relieving himself, overhears the inmates' wise words. Even if he doesn't fully understand their way of speaking, he gets the overall picture. There he is, grasping the kettle without saying a word; he gives a firm knock at the door. The jailer opens the hatch. "What's going on?" The old worker points to the kettle, too big to go through the hatch and says in a perfectly natural tone of voice, "Go and get us some water, son!" A few minutes later, the jailer puts the kettle on the floor and opens the door, "There you go!" Immediately a line of thirsty figures form, led by the wisemen.

YEZHOV

I was most familiar with his name before my arrest in Moscow in 1937. He was the Minister of the Interior of the USSR, more precisely the People's Commissar of Internal Affairs as it was called at the time. Every day the media would praise him for his fight against the enemy of the people— those counter-revolutionary vermin who prevented us from marching towards a better future. I remember Boris Efimov's drawings showing "Yezhov, the Stalinist minister" slaying this scum. One of the drawings showed the enemy of the people strangled by a powerful fist with a glove in the shape of a hedgehog (*yezh* means "hedgehog" in Russian). Every day the newspapers would release the names of the new traitors who had just been identified.

We were a group of young Communists, all foreigners, staying in a dacha near Moscow. We were all convinced that only the Communist Revolution would achieve social justice in the world by following Lenin's undertakings as pursued by his genial and unwavering follower, Stalin. Didn't we say, "Stalin is today's Lenin?" Yet, two of our comrades couldn't understand how Zinoviev—Lenin's faithful companion, the brilliant and dedicated leader of the Comintern— could possibly betray the cause. They quickly disappeared and no-one ever heard of them again.

Here I am in Butyrka Prison. I am apprehensive but deeply convinced that this "mistake" will be cleared up. It lasted over twenty years which enabled me to understand, among other things, that Yezhov was not the noble fighter of a hypothetical scum but a cynical and cruel executioneer and, even worse, he had been so on Stalin's orders, and not in the name of Marxism-Leninism, which was my ideal.

After barely two years in power he slaughtered millions of people, most ot them innocent victims accused of crimes they had never committed, and Yezhov disappeared without a trial... something common on Soviet terrain, also known as "the liquidation of the liquidators." Embarrassing witnesses had to disappear. It was a fixed rule. Yezhov was probably aware of that and knew there was no way out.

Years later, somewhere in Siberia, on one of the many convoys and transfers, I found myself sharing a cell with a man who had been to the same school as Yezhov as a child. When he arrived in Moscow from his remote village in the mid-thirties, he went and sought after his old classmate and became an important executive of the Communist Party. Yezhov had greeted him cordially, had gotten him a good position, the same for his wife and, even better, had given them a beautiful apartment, a most extraordinary privilege. Yezhov was not yet minister under Stalin.

SOCIALIST LEGALITY

There has never been any formal *legality* throughout the seventy-three years of Communist dictatorship in Russia, only *Socialist legality* was allowed (1).

We are in 1937, in the heat of Stalinist terror. Over a million men and women have been executed, all of them after quick show trials, most behind closed doors. A secret instruction from the party indicates that the prisoners must be tried and condemned after they confess to crimes they have never committed. It follows that the use of torture is perfectly legal. The party, nonetheless, only deals with serious cases of national importance. It won't deal with trivial things.

During a routine search, one of the jailers discovers in my stuff some left-over bread rations, cut into slices. He fills out a report he insists that I sign which states "cut with a knife." I refuse. Knives are prohibited in prison camps. I am aware of it. The latter is taken by surprise by my refusal and knows perfectly well that one can extract signatures through torture for far more petty offences and that this is all in accordance with the party's regulations. Now, are there any instructions, though, for such a petty offence? Without the signature of the jailer, there won't be any report and therefore no punishment. Thus, for merely administrative reasons, while thousands of people were shot, I managed that one time to avoid the cooler.

NOTES
(1) Following the feeble attempt to condemn Stalin's "cult of personality," the monthly newspaper *Partininaia Jizn* [*The Party Life*] in its April 1957 issue mentioned "measures taken to reinforce legality and strict respect of the citizen's rights." It was the only case in the Russian Communist dictatorship in which the concept of *legality* in itself was ever mentioned... and it didn't last long.

GOD MOVES IN MYSTERIOUS WAYS

A bright light hurts my pupils. I hear a loud crash. I slowly and painfully wake up. Everyone gets up in the middle of the night and the "flyers" (1) are folded up. It is either a search or a "cell disbandment" (a prison security measure to prohibit development of friendly groups among prisoners—unity makes strength!—in pretrial prisons). For me it is a novelty, whereas my fellow inmates are accustomed to it.

As I am emerging from my little corner right on the ground, under the bedboards, bumping into my neighbours, I see Lago-Ozerov. Half asleep, he is wrapping his cock with a long thread in the vague hope of covering it before the search. I am stunned by his natural dignity in such a ludicrous situation. The day before he reminisced about Paris and his coming to the rescue of a girl who had attempted suicide on the Pont Neuf in the middle of the night. He has been working on this for two days, patiently pulling out the thread of his beautiful socks that came from Paris. He needs it to tie up his pants since all of his buttons were removed upon his arrival in the prison, as per the camp regulations.

A few minutes later, the hatch opens and the jailer calls ten names in an undertone. Well, it is no search but indeed a "cell disbandment," else we would all have been marched off. The hatch closes and the door opens. Ten exit in silence. The same scenario repeats several times. I am with the last group, so is Lago-Ozerov. As soon as the door is shut behind us, one of the three guards, with a voucher in his hand, counts the ten of us in an undertone, checks our identity and orders us to "proceed forward" along the corridor. From time to time we would hear his brief commands, "To the left!" "To the right!" "Halt!" Every couple of metres we have to stop before going through another gate, then upstairs, to more hallways, until we finally reach another section and face another cell door. The jailer checks the form that the cell duty officer hands him and shows us in.

Our arrival in the cell wakes up its occupants. Only the *staroste* (2), all sleepy, gets up and tells us to lie down on the lower bed boards, the only ones available. Men adjust themselves, complaining in their sleep. Everyone manages to find their spot and falls asleep. Once asleep, reveille is sounded. We get to know the "natives." Just like us—the "outsiders"—they crave to hear about what's going on (there is no newspaper circulating in the prison) and what's happened to people who received the same sentence as theirs. The administration of Butyrka Prison has to be most inventive in forbidding such encounters.

Then there comes the time of the daily bread distribution, given with the two lumps of sugar and religious silence. Conversations then resume, still in undertone. In the crowd I spot a handsome fellow of Eastern descent. His elegant clothes are worn through. He has been evidently sleeping on the lower berths for many years. His name is Rachid. He is a courteous fellow. He's an Afghani who sought political asylum in the Soviet Union. Although he was no Communist, he was against the king, Zahir Shah. In the midst of this multitude dumbfounded by their misfortune, he seems quite detached: this horrible tragedy affects Russia and not his country. Little does he know that half a century later Moscow—after imposing its regime on almost all nearby countries—would fight a war against Afghanistan and, because the invader failed to colonize it, the Soviet Union would end up withdrawing after leaving the country devastated. Rachid is most philosophical about his personal mishap. He has been here five years, already. Lago-Ozerov would explain to me later that the NKVD would keep people "on hand" for years whom they might consider using one day to instigate some politically "relevant" provocation. Indeed, thirteen years later I met Prince Konoe Fumitaka—son of the former Japanese Prime-Minister (3)—at the end of the immense Gulag empire. After spending seven or eight years in a pre-trial prison, the (NKVD) political police had finally given up the idea of using him in some completely fabricated trial, and instead had sentenced him to twenty-five years of prison. Once imprisoned, more time could always be added on.

As for Lago-Ozerov, I found out much later that he belonged to INO, the Foreign Department involved with espionage abroad (part of the OGPU-NKVD). He was imprisoned in Butyrka straight from Paris, where he had been resident courtesy of the Soviet Secret Services. Another one of those swallowed up by the Great Purge.

One last detail: one day during one of the many millions of transfers I was subjected to, I ran into an old cell-mate from my first cell at Butyrka. He was happily surprised to see me alive. He had seen Lago-Ozerov, who, as a former superior executive from the NKVD, had said that presumably someone like Jacques Rossi had been shot; we all imagined that Lago-Ozerov would never escape a bullet in the neck either. There were hundreds of thousands of suspects executed without any justification whatsoever. It simply shows that God moves in mysterious ways, just like the NKVD.

NOTES
(1) The "flyers" are sleeping panels made out of three planks or bed boards, set up in the overcrowded cells to fill the space between two rows of continuous bed boards located along the opposite walls of a cell, thus accomodating more people.

(2) Cell representative.

(3) In 1945 following Hiroshima, although the country was already on its knees, the Soviet Union declared war on Japan. The whole Manchurian Army, including Lieutenant Konoe Fumitaka, were taken prisoner without putting up a fight.

SZMUL SZWARC

What strikes me about him are his big brown sad eyes, reflecting astonishment. He must be eighteen and looks lost in this overcrowded hellhole of a barracks which, after curfew, the camp administration fills up with more and more people. After much swearing and beating, everyone has managed to find themselves a spot. Paralysed, he doesn't budge. His woollen hat is inapproriately placed. What an oddball! I am intrigued. "Where do you come from?" His sad astonished eyes look into mine. "Warsaw." " *Mòwisz po polsku?* You speak Polish?" "Yes, I do." I find out that his father is a hatter in the Jewish quarter in Warsaw. Because of the Soviet-German pact between Fascist Germany and Communist Russia that enabled Hitler to declare World War II a few weeks ago, his family had to flee to escape Hitler's armies. Once on the Soviet side, they were quickly separated and each one of them deported to a different labor camp. He has no clue as to where his father, his mother, his two sisters, and little brother are.

My new acquaintance, Szmul Swarc (to be pronounced Schmul Schwartz), is just at the beginning of his calvary. Mine started two years ago and I am ten years older than him. As a "vet" I find him a spot to lie down. Tomorrow there will be reveille at five in the morning, followed by the bread distribution, the meager soup and then we'll be off to work for eleven and a half hours straight (1). He is assigned to another brigade than mine but manages to come and see me from time to time, and each time I try to give him some insight about this universe I myself am becoming more familiar with. If his Russian is quite basic—he's learnt it on his own—his Polish is most eloquent. He has just graduated from highschool in Warsaw. The language and his stories of Poland bring us together. He seems to consider me an older brother.

Then we got separated because of a work assignment. It wasn't until years later that I found out that, at the time I was in the cooler—quite a common thing!—Szmul had tried to pass on a bread ration to me and it turned out it was his. He was so naive that it never occurred to him it was bound to have been stolen. Sixty years have gone by and, up till now, I will be ever grateful to Szmul for his amazing and inconceivably generous gesture.

NOTES
(1) On June 1941 following Germany's attack on the USSR, the workday went from 10 hours to 11 1/2 hours.

LE LOUVRE

Four in the morning. The hatch opens. There are about thirty of us in a cell, all shorn, wearing striped pyjamas. Some don't sleep, tormented by their thoughts. Behind the hatch, the guard whispers: "Letter A!" "Alexandrov." "Another one?" "Androuchenko." "Another one?" "Abramovitch." "First name, first name of the father, birthdate, article, sentence, end of term?" The old Abramovitch answers each question. Everything matches. "Get ready with your belongings!" The hatch closes. Abramovitch gets dressed. The door opens to let him out and is closed behind him.

They insist on this process because thanks to this complex ritual, those in one cell are prevented from learning about the presence of another prisoner in another cell should the guard state the last name and be at the wrong cell. Prison rules forbid prisoners from knowing anything about their co-detainees in other cells. Fifteen minutes later the same ritual repeats itself. This time, it's the letter B. In two hours eight people left the cell, one by one. I am the last to go. It is already six in the morning. The jailer takes me to solitary confinement. I am searched by someone else. He doesn't find anything, not even the least fragment of metal or lead (like a pin, for example). All is good. He locks me up. My fellow inmates before me must all be in individual cells too, kept secret. Each one of us hears doors open and shut, people pacing the hallways, but we have no idea who it could be. Everything is performed in silence. The official purpose of this is to hand the prisoners their mail, if they have any. We call this "to read letters." De facto, each prisoner is entitled to receive and read one letter per month unless he is forbidden to correspond following a disciplinary measure or upon special instruction from within the hierarchy. If he has received more than one, the security officer only hands him one. The others will wait. Sometimes the security officer would let the prisoner pick one—an act of kindness maybe not genuine—the prisoner won't brag about it. Only letters from their families (parents, children, brothers and sisters as long as they are in the prisoner's personal file) are given out. Grandparents, cousins, grandchildren and friends are excluded. Besides, prisoners are allowed to send only one letter every six months. It's forbidden for those whose families live abroad, unless there is a special instruction.

Around eleven o'clock it's my turn. The escort orders me to stop in front of the security officer's door. He adjusts his uniform, puts on a serious look and knocks at the door. "Come in!" "Comrade lieutenant-colonel, the detainee is at your disposal, according to your orders!" The officer dismisses him and as soon as the door is shut he says, "There is no mail for you. Do you have any questions?" I have been hearing this every month for years. Since I have no family in the USSR I am not allowed to correspond with anyone. As for the questions, he is the one who is asking them.

The ritual of "reading letters" enables the security officer to see individually every month each one of the three or four hundred detainees of the prison. It is also a way to find out about what is going on in the cells. How many times did he surprise us by quoting the exact words or gestures of one of us? He seems to know everything, including insignificant details, and the awareness of us being exposed twenty four hours a day to this infernal vigilance terrorises us and makes us crazy.

Between nine and noon each of us has a personal interview with the security officer. Everything is designed to prevent us from knowing how long they last. It is believed that the one who spends the most time of all is an informer. After this first visit, each prisoner is taken back to the same solitary cell. Those who have received mail read it. The rest spend their time as they can. Then between 3:00 pm and 6:00 pm there is a second visit to the security officer, always one on one. Those who received mail return it to him for inclusion in their personal file. The officer may even add a confidential note to it. After that, prisoners are returned to their solitary cells, only taken back to our original cell, "ours," late in the night around 2:00 am or 3:00 am.

During one of those rituals, I find the security officer to be pretty relaxed. After the same old, "You have no mail," he asks that I tell him about Paris , its monuments and brothels he's read about. He is most interested in the Louvre. I am impressed to see that even a KGB lieutenant-colonel from Siberia, the end of the world, knows about Le Louvre! My memories resurface from a most unreal past of the Venus de Milo, the Joconda, but that's not what the officer is interested in. "Tell me, isn't it at the Louvre that you can see the famous couple from Pompei embracing, caught in lava?" At that very moment, the escort whom he had called just before by ringing a bell, knocks at the door. The officer immediately stops talking, tells him to come and orders him abruptly to take me back to my cell.

He, the most feared man of the prison, from the last of the detainees to the camp director himself whose assistant he is—he, the dreaded and almighty representative of the State Police, doesn't dare take the risk to have a lowly private witness such an unexpected interrogation.

BECAUSE MAN'S HANDS ARE LIKE THIS

It was the third time our paths had crossed each other. The first time we were in the hold of a barge. We were more than a thousand prisoners, packed like sardines, heading to the north. After seventeen or eighteen days we got off on a deserted shore of the Arctic tundra. That's Norilsk Forced Labor Camp. I had the frightening sensation of being projected to the other end of the world, cut from anything, whereas many of my companions in misery wouldn't let this new misfortune affect them—one amongst many. One man, particularly, stood out. He had a bushy grey beard. He remained indifferent. I found him three years later in a brigade of ditch-diggers, looking his old self: calm and unmoved. I was impressed by the way he handled the pickaxe and the crowbar. I was able to find out his name at the prisoner count, Semione Ievlampievitch.

Many years later here we are sleeping on the ground, squeezed under the boards of a disciplinary barracks. The berths are taken by the hoods and the thieves, as is the rule. We exchange news. I find out that before October 1917 Revolution Semione Ievlampievitch was part of the "Tolstoyans," a somewhat unclear organization of peasants influenced by the teachings of Tolstoy. His first experience in the Gulag dates back to the 30s, during the forced collectivization. Once he was freed he was swallowed by the Great Purge of 1937 and sentenced to ten years in forced labor camp.

He immediately saw in me the foreigner, the rich kid, and a Communist on top of everything. In his great generosity, not only does he not hold any grudge, but he explains indulgently that the Marxist-Leninist ideal is a wild and impossible dream. Why? Because man's hands are made like this... they're constantly pulling things towards him.

THE CHINESE KOMSOMOL

I strive to recall my Chinese, "*Ni che tsung nâ-li laï-de jen?*" ("Where are you from?") Apparently surprised, the man stares at me without saying a word, then suspicious, asks, "Have you been to China?" We are inside a large room filled with people in the transit prison of Novosibirsk. I am with a group of fifteen prisoners recently transferred from the transit prison of Krasnoiarsk. We do not know our destination. I try to find a place in this multitude, another one in my enforced wanderings, and manage to find a narrow space between two bodies. One looks Chinese, I don't know about the other. He smells strongly. I carry on talking to the Chinese man and say, "More than twenty years ago I went through Shanghai and I have been in the Gulag since 1937." He doesn't talk much. I find out that he is from North-East China and has been in the USSR for twenty-seven years, twenty-six of them in the Gulag. I don't ask him the silly question, "For what reason?" I know very well that there are only two reasons for winding up in the Gulag: Firstly, when there is a suspicion of a suspicion; secondly, any other excuse.

All of a sudden the door opens and the security officer appears, a form in his hand. All conversations immediately stop. There are sixty pairs of eyes riveted to him. He reads out a dozen names and each one gives their first name, their father's first name, birthdate, article of the penal code, sentence, end of term. The officer checks the list, all is in order, and commands, "Get your belongings!" and exits. The door is shut then reopens a few moments later. Men are escorted off, one by one, with their bundle. My Chinese friend is amongst them. I have memorized his name, Li.

Six weeks go by and hundreds of men come and go through our transit cell, arriving from various camps and prisons of the gigantic Gulag empire. Some arrive, others leave, no-one knows where to. It is my turn to be transferred and I wind up in the transit prison of Sverdlovsk. Once all the rituals are completed, my brigade is led to a large room. As always it is overcrowded and the only spots available are right on the ground covered with juicy spit that look like soft oysters. I find a spot that is not too soiled. A man comes to me, it's Li! This time he tells me his personal story.

He was a soldier in the Chiang-Kai-Chek's army in 1929, based near the USSR border and there were often skirmishes between the Soviets and the Chinese. Li was part of the underground cell of young Communists of his unit. When they found out about an imminent sneak attack on the Soviet army, the young Communists decided to warn their Russian brothers. Li managed to circumvent the vigilance of the Chinese guardposts and miraculously escaped the Soviet bullets by crossing a no man's land and succeeded in being escorted to the commander. The latter didn't in the least suspect the presence of a Chinese detachment. He summoned his officers and asked Li to show him on an ordinance survey map the exact position of his detachment. Li complied and was to ready to leave, eager to warn his Communist comrades to flee before the Russian assault. But the commander insisted that he eat something and so there was Li seated at the Soviet officers' table, being served a meal accompanied with lots of vodka.

Li woke up the next day suffering a migraine and found out his whole unit had been wiped out by Russian artillery.

This anecdote brought back some old memories. In 1929, twenty-seven years earlier, during my first stay in the USSR, I had found myself travelling with some young Soviet Communists as devoted as myself. One of them was from Asia, and was an officer of the Red Army, who recounted that same incident with great detail. It turns out that he was the commander Li had met. I was shocked and deeply moved by the whole thing. How can one possibly massacre some comrades abroad in cold blood who are struggling to achieve world revolution? "The Soviet Union's interest comes before the Communist International Party!" insisted the commander. "What guarantees would we have had, if by joining his unit, Li wouldn't have betrayed them under torture? Besides, he added, don't you forget, comrade, that all of this must remain top secret." Decades later in 1991, during his last intervention before the Supreme Soviet, Andrei Sakharov would protest against the practice of the Soviet Armies in Afghanistan. In cases where it was impossible to evacuate groups of soldiers surrounded by Mujahideen, Russian commanders would systematically send helicopters to massacre them. Always the same old concern: preventing the enemy from having access to the smallest piece of information.

HUNGER

The folds of my empty stomach lining are contracting and rubbing against each other. Not the slightest bit of food to keep them apart. It is as if they want to devour each other. I am not sure if that's what's happening but that's how it feels. It is a nagging pain that only sleep can relieve. In the Gulag there is a saying, "The prisoner's sleep is sacred. It is good for his nerves and gives him a sense of not being hungry."

I am hungry. I have been for years. I know perfectly well that it's never going to change. Never. Hunger torments one's mind as one's stomach. I feel I'm losing my grip. Confused memories emerge from the distant past, of the free world before I arrived in the Soviet Union, before my arrival in the Gulag... memories of determined fights for social justice, liberty, and so on. We are five or six young devoted activists talking about how to change the world. Everyone quotes Marx, Engels, Lenin. The world revolution is just around the corner. It is inevitable. We are sitting at a table with some left-overs of dinner: scraps of white bread (!) hardly touched, chicken drumsticks with some meat left on them, glasses with drops of wine at the bottom. I strive not to think about this crazy mirage. At no cost should one allow such "gastronomic masturbation," an expression used in the Gulag to describe our gastronomic *souvenirs*. Its consequence is to weaken the resistance of the starving convict that the almighty political police of the almighty Communist dictatorship is already determined to break. Let us not make it easy for them!

I am now strolling along the Champs Elysées. The weather is nice. I pass some beautiful shop windows, cafés, bars, I see happy people sitting around... No! Not again! *This time I am taking a walk in the Louvre. The Winged Victory of Samothrace, the Venus de Milo, the divine Joconda, and nearby the Flemish paintings with Rubens and his exuberant representations of human flesh, some still-lifes with heaps of delicious enticing food...* Oh no! To hell with those souvenirs! There is no escape. Even if I were to swallow my six hundred grams of rye bread in one gulp – the daily ration of an inmate – hunger remains. The stealing of bread in the barracks by fellow prisoners was commonplace, only prevented by shovelling it down one's throat. One learns this quickly. Though the bread is all sticky from the humidity, only occasionally you might be able to grill it on the stove. Then it becomes crusty, and when you put it into your mouth and chew for a very long time, it becomes sweet. Simply delicious. Never mind if one of your neighbours is getting rid of his lice and throwing them into the same wooden stove; they burn and crack like fireworks.

It is mostly in the central prisons, where one is incarcerated twenty four hours a day, that there is time to "ruminate" indefinitely over the smallest piece of bread, the slightest grain of millet porridge. Of course it doesn't apply to those who work at the canteen who can eat whatever they want. How hard it is for the outcasts not to look their way, not to hear their chewing and burping. How difficult it is to reason with oneself that the lump of sugar your neighbour has isn't (nor can be) bigger than yours.

It is true that the Gulag enables its convicts to improve their daily ration thanks to an additional effort. Alas, the norm is such that the additional bread cannot under any circumstances compensate for the extra exertion required. The prisoner inevitably weakens and becomes a garbage picker. Hence the saying, "It isn't the small bread ration that will kill you, it is the large one."

COLD

Imagine a giant drawing a pail of water in a river of light and projecting that same light in a dash against the firmament. Neon-like pale splashes blink here and there all around the sky dome. Rays that undulate, shake, zigzag, jump, switch off, just to suddenly reappear somewhere else. Sometimes it is a huge curtain of light, high in the sky, wavering just like the *aurora borealis* from my childhood geography book of a million years ago when I was a child. My goodness! It is so high! Here, the look of this amazing natural phenomenon doesn't excite any of us in the least. The sky must be completely clear in order to see the aurora borealis. It is already -40°C, and any further drop in temperature will be felt immediately. No need for a thermometer. It is as if our bones were freezing. When it is -50°C, one has to make an effort to prevent eyelids from sticking together and every time one takes a breath, it is as if knives were piercing your lungs.

You protect yourselves as well as possible by tightening cuffs at the wrists above your mittens with a piece of string; same thing for the ankles. Instead of a belt, another piece of string is used to prevent the glacial air from penetrating the clothes. You pull your hat all the way down to your eyebrows, wrap a rag around your neck to cover everything except the eyes. Your breath forms a crust of ice which freezes and cuts the bridge of your nose. Some leave their nose uncovered, risking that it will freeze. They never stop blowing on the drop that forms at the end of their runny nose. No possible use for a handkerchief. Taking one's mitten off to dig into one's pocket is practically impossible. Fingers instantly turn numb. It is already difficult enough to button one's pants after taking a pee. All these basic tasks are time consuming. From the underwear to the quilted jacket and pants, the stockings, the sailor's duffle coat and the hat, all the clothes are made of cotton. On top of stockings, the prisoners wear shoes made out of woven rope. Only once per hour can we get close to the fires but for no more than five minutes. Watch out for the sparks! Cotton catches fire easily, unlike the guards' coats which are made out of sheepskin and their solid felt boots. We are jealous of their red, well-fed faces. They are the ones who made us light the fires they remain close to, with the exception of the few minutes we are granted.

In the 1920s, labor outdoors—except for emergency work—had to stop when the temperature reached 25°C below. Later on, per some secretive instructions, they raised the threshold to 50°C below, like in the Kolyma, for example. The convicts served as guinea pigs for the Soviet power to test human resistance to cold, hunger, poor treatment and so on. The results thus obtained were way below the figures set by the Worldwide Health Organization. Another world record shattered!

REVEILLE

Several blows on the iron rail signal reveille in the distance. The metallic noise carried out in the glacial air of the night resembles the sound of pure crystal in the stinky overcrowded barracks. It is five in the morning. It's pitch dark. The night will last many more months still, this is winter beyond the Arctic Circle, in Siberia.

For us it is the beginning of a new day. There are a hundred and twenty-five men in half of our barracks, all pressed against each other on two-tier bedboards. These are planks fixed to the wall on the sides, all the way along the length of the barracks, one of them at fifty centimeters and the other at a meter-ten from the ground. When getting up, those who sleep on the lower bedboards often hit their heads against the feet of those who are above them, provoking swearing and fights. It is already so hard to try to awaken from the sleep that makes us forget about hunger.

Before reveille, Vano, the orderly, went to get our overcoats, our shoes and our Russian socks (those straps of fabric Russians wrap their feet with using them as socks) that were drying off in a special spot. All of our things are grey, shapeless, and a hundred times mended. All we can see of Vano, carrying this enormous bundle of rags, are his feet. Before he even drops them on the floor we rush to him to retrieve our stuff. Not an easy task. Russian socks are difficult to identify. You can never find your pair, and often wind up taking someone else's. More fights and beatings.

The wash stands are installed in the passageway that divides the structure into two sections, leading to the outside-door. The temperature inside is almost the same as outside. Water is frozen from October to mid-May. Inside the barracks there is a barrel filled with water that doesn't freeze. Some astute inmates fill their mouths with that water before going through the passageway and let it run in their hands, using them as makeshift-washbasins. Others only wait for a bath, once every ten days, preceded by the mandatory shaving of the head and the pubis (the beard is optional); all of this is done with the same trimmer.

In the meantime, Vano made a new appearance, this time with two pails of hot water for breakfast. Very few remember having had coffee or tea in the morning. Then comes the most solemn moment of the day: Vano comes back from the baker's with our bread. He went to get it with an escort of strong guys from our brigade to avoid being robbed on the way out. All went well. Here are our precious bread rations piled up on his straw mattress. With envy, we savour its gooey reddishness. We get high on its tart smell. The rations weigh from four hundred fifty grams to nine hundred grams, water amounting to half of the bread. Their number and weight are carefully set according to the report of the brigadier, who has specified with minute detail the norm fulfilled during each individual's work-shift.

This bread is the staple of our diet. It is the most vital element. In the Gulag, it is also the most stable currency, just like the US Dollar in third-world countries. Once bread distribution is over, the hot meals, soup and porridge (usually millet) are served. Once this is over, we get ready for work. Everyone pulls their quilted hat down on their heads, ties the ear flaps, wraps a piece of cloth tightly around their necks, then puts on their overcoat, buttoning it well and tightening it up at the waist with a piece of string, same for the wrists and ankles. The ritual takes a lot of time and care, especially for the right wrist! We look like peasants harnessing their horses except that here, we are the horses. Years later, when I saw on television astronauts donning their space suits, it reminded me of our meticulous preparation.

We are ready to work ten to twelve hours outside in a temperature below 40°C. Vano will stay in the barracks to clean and protect our few belongings as well as possible. (Vano is the barrack keeper and won't work outdoor.) Like all the inmates forced to work, we do his share.

It's 6:00 am. The signal sounds. All the barracks disgorge multitudes of exhausted, worn out, grey inmates. Resigned, they march off to the gate where armed guards with dogs escort them to the worksite. Altogether we shall contribute a new stone to the radiant Communist monument.

OFF TO WORK!

It is winter. It is not 6:00 am yet. The gate of the compound is closed. Well "gate" is a big word. It is simply a wooden frame with horizontal and diagonal barbed wire. We can see the escort guards with their dogs. They are the ones to march us off to our respective worksites. We have already been lined up in brigades formed of five each. Many brigadiers get together. Most of them are non-political prisoners: the work assigner with a list of all brigades departing for work, with indication of their assignment to sites, their rosters and the number of people; a camp policeman, a free man, with his personnel, all non-political inmates; a staff member from the Administrative and Supply Unit. If an inmate complains about the tattered clothes he was given being unable to withstand the harsh conditions, or feels he is being underfed to sustain work, they answer him that "he has been fed and dressed according to the season." He then has the choice between the cooler or the worksite. A chief from the Cultural and Educational Unit is also there. For the umpteenth time he will be surprised to witness the true lack of enthusiasm of those forced labor convicts of Socialism—as opposed to the widespread official propaganda. The presence of the medical orderly, particularly, is most touching: if a convict is incapacitated because of a serious illness, he will give him a pill. Indeed there is a regulation that sets the quota of those exempt from work at 6% and that quota is often officially met. It is no coincidence that there is a saying, "You will be exempt from work only with your head under your arm." The chief of the forced labor camp hardly ever attends the whole ceremony and may ask his representative to be present. As for the most important character in the camp—the security officer—he doesn't need to be present since he is kept fully informed about everything thanks to his vast network of informers.

6:00 am. The signal to march off to work is given. The guards fling the gates open. One of them holds a piece of plywood. He gives a nod to the brigadier of the brigade closest to the gates who in turn gives his last name, Petrov. He finds his name on his piece of plywood and orders the brigade to move on through. They go through the gate in their rows of five. The two guards count them: "First, second, third…" multiply by five, add the number of people in the last incomplete row plus the brigadier, and supply the resultant sum by saying out loud: "Petrov Brigade, twenty-nine men." The guard enters the figure on his plywood followed by the name of Petrov. Sometimes the guards miscount the inmates, and then the brigade has to turn around and be counted again. The escort guard and his personnel then count them again. They make mistakes too. The marching off of thirty brigades i.e. from six to seven hundred men may take more than one hour, no matter what weather conditions, whether it rains, freezes or if there's wind. The exact same procedure applies to their return from their ten hourwork day.

Hundreds of men have already marched off when all of a sudden a prisoner breaks the monotony of the procession. As Sidorenko's brigade was going through the gates, one prisoner stripped his clothes until he was naked. His eyes were shining. He looked as if he was possessed. Everyone knows that a prisoner who is not "dressed according to the season" would not be accepted by the escort, and this man is the sole decision-maker, not having to rely on the camp chief. The police chief nodded at his men, who immediately dragged the poor soul aside by the arms and tossed him in the snow. The recount of the brigades resumed as if nothing had happened. Every time the man tried to raise his head, the policemen would stick it in the ground and continue kicking him, not too violently though. It wasn't until the last team went by that they would order him to get up and get dressed. If he had refused, he would be taken away, completely naked. What's surprising is that this incident rarely leads to pneumonia. Later on he would have to sign the sentence condemning him to ten days in the cooler with forced labor. Nonetheless he would be spared a long walk barefoot to his team's worksite, and working in the camp compound is less hard. There, one feels a bit "at home."

As for the brigades that march off to work, sometimes they might see one or more corpses lying on the ground outside the gates. These are escapees who were caught and beaten to death by the escort who doesn't like anyone to part from him. Their bodies will remain there several days perhaps; it is an old tradition that goes back to the 1920s, and like any old institution, the Gulag remains most attached to its traditions.

A SPRING DAY

"Step to the left! Step to the right! The escort will fire without warning! Understood?" "Understood!" we respond altogether, in a monotone, without thinking. That's the warning from the escort guard after he's counted us a number of times when exiting the camp. We have heard this formula a thousand times, acknowledged by our response, "Understood," like an "amen." We call it "the prayer"— a most unusual one because we have seen some of our fellow inmates shot for stepping out.

The escort now orders us to march off to work. There are more than four kilometers ahead of us. It is the end of May. The Arctic sun no longer goes down. Twenty-four hours a day its warm rays lick the snow accumulated from eight months of winter. However, the ever frozen ground—permafrost—miles deep, remains impervious. The tundra turns into an ocean of mud. With every step, we must make an effort to remove our legs from the sucking mud. We keep on slipping, falling, getting up again, and we have to mind our pathetic army boots. We are exhausted from years of malnourishment and the relentlessness of hard labor exceeding our physical strength. Our legs are numb from the accumulated fatigue. Strangely enough, after a hard day at work, they feel more relaxed. Is it because we are "going back home" or because our muscles warmed up on the worksite? As for our escort guards, well fed, rested, warmly dressed with proper shoes, they stride ahead purposefully. They don't seem to mind the mud. They scream their heads off, "Move on through! March off! No stragglers!" One of them plays with the bolt of his gun in my back. Has he loaded a bullet into his gun? I don't care. If I continue to walk it's only because I am afraid of being on my own, isolated from my fellow inmates.

We finally see the worksite. We are completely exhausted and need to get our tools from the hut— pickaxes, iron crowbars, shovels, etc. Some of my fellow inmates look for a specific shovel or pickaxe. They have experience. They know which tools are the easiest to handle. How? Well, "You ain't at university! You've got to think!"

Once we have our tools we march of to the worksite. We need to dig foundations. The ground is hard as cement. Where it has been hit with iron crowbars and pickaxes it has turned into mud thanks to the spring sun. Those who dig at the end of the pit trudge through deep mud mixed with rocks and pebbles. Some shovel out the mud which others load onto wheelbarrows which are then taken to the dump. Once they are emptied, they are brought back and so on. We have set up tracks by putting together wooden planks—to be able to push the wheelbarrows, we prevent the wheel from sliding onto the rough and muddy terrain. Accidents can be a major issue for the brigade because they cause a decrease in output which inevitably affects the bread ration. Unlike worksites anywhere else in the world, the Gulag does not hire professional or skilled workers but uses only those sent by the state police. Amongst us there is a barber, a professor specialised in Marxist philosophy, two officers, three peasants, a young delinquent, three Communist apparatchiks, one singer from the Novosibirsk Opera and a few manual workers (railwaymen, miners, etc). Some are more efficient than others and they are the ones who can secure the rations. They are the same ones who exert psychological and sometimes physical abuse on the "weaker ones," i.e., those recognized as physically incapable. Such abuse, when it lasts years, is as trying as the material conditions of the camp. Yet, its effects on you is evidence that the Gulag has not yet completely crushed you.

"YOU, YOU AND YOU!!"

"You, you and you! Over here!" We are over three hundred convicts, crouched down, hands on our heads, surrounded by armed
escorts. For eighteen days we had been locked up in Krasnoiarsk,
two thousand kilometers upstream, in the holds of a barge. They are
now transferring us to the forced labor camp of Norilsk, beyond the
Arctic Circle.

"You, you and you! Over here!" A guard checks us, speaking in
a dry tone, scrutinizing one individual in particular with a piercing
eye and pointing at him with his finger. He gets up without resistance and picks up his bundle. After a while another group of convicts
gather. They will be transferred somewhere else. Some of their faces
are engrained in my memory. After ten years in Norilsk Camp I will
run into some of them, all are hardened criminals, thieves through
and through, like Crater-Face Grichka or Ruptured Eye Jorka. It
wasn't the first time that I was able to admire how the guards had
a photographic memory for their faces, same as the criminals had.

A NAIL STUCK IN BETWEEN BALLS

The secretary to the chief of the prison camp, whose job is to protect his superior from unwelcoming individuals, allows Ruptured-Eye Jorka in with no problem. "Good morning, captain citizen!" says Jorka. "Here is the daily report on the activities of the camp bakery." Interrupting his assistant, who is explaining a project about connecting electricity to the barbed wire, the captain reaches out and grabs the large envelope Jorka hands him. The latter says goodbye, is dismissed and exits.

Jorka, a thug condemned many times for murder, is in charge of the bakery. It is a most lucrative and cushy job, as long as he cuts in the captain... hence the envelope full of banknotes.

Much to the Captain's dismay, lately Jorka has been too greedy, and now he's trying to find a way to get rid of him. It is not a simple task. The easiest way would be to surprise him with a transfer to another camp. Those transfers or convoys are organized by professionals: the list of prisoners is set up secretly and communicated just as secretly to the transfer services. They are the ones who organize a true military operation: in a few minutes the camp is surrounded and the transferred prisoners taken by the soldiers. There is no escape... except for an old veteran of the Gulag like Ruptured-Eye Jorka, who knows the ropes. He takes his pants down, sits on the ground, pulls out a nail from his pocket, which he had been saving for such a specific instance, and sticks it in between his balls. There he is, stuck to the floor. In order to get him out of that position, a locksmith is required and, given the circumstances, a nurse. The transfer services, which run independently of the chief of the forced labor camp, have very strict instructions to follow. In such a case, the individual's name must be crossed out from the list and the convoy leave without him. The poor Captain has to find another way to get rid of Ruptured-Eye Jorka.

"YOU'RE PERFECTLY SAFE"

Crater-Face Grichka was contemplating the scrap of paper he was holding by the tips of his fingers. It was actually just a piece of a bag of cement, roughly cleaned, with his penciled portrait scribbled on it. Behaving according to the thieves' code, he said nothing, but was obviously pleased, and the hoodlums of his court started praising this "work of art" at random. Artistic considerations were put aside to appreciate the "resemblance" between the model and portrait. It was so difficult to tell the difference between the two that Ruptured-Eye Jorka would speak to the portrait as if it were the person, "Oh you are so handsome, Grichka! What a proud look you have! All the girls must be crazy about you!" The author of the famous portrait was none other than me. I was most proud of it.

"Don't you fear anything, you pigeon! You're perfectly safe here," he said to me in a protective tone, ordering one of his assistants to give me a ration of bread. My Goodness! A bread ration weighing seven hundred and fifty grams. I was too hungry to question where it came from. I completely trusted Crater-Face Grichka's words. Nothing, absolutely nothing, would happen on his territory without his knowledge. As a matter of fact, I never ran into any problems while he was still alive. But thieves don't last forever.

Years later, in 1949, the Kremlin protested Norway joining NATO. "It is a known fact that Norway is perfectly safe, so it doesn't need to join." That was a typical Crater-Face Grichka comment and a great lesson in Kremlinology.

THE ESCAPE

Ivan Petrov succeeded... Everyone is happy for him. He managed to escape the supervigilance of the overpowerful Soviet police and flee the forced labor camp of Norilsk, above the Arctic Circle. He is about fifty years old, a former accountant, sentenced to ten years in prison for counter-revolutionary crimes. He was first transferred in June with other prisoners from Krasnoiarsk, where he was originally from, as soon as the River Yenisei had become navigable. And then disappeared in September, as the river prepared to freeze for a long period.

More than one year has gone by. We haven't had any news. One day, one of his friends arrives in a transfer and tells us that, thanks to the complicity of a sailor who had killed someone and whom he blackmailed, Ivan managed to sail up the Yenisei until Krasnoiarsk in the hold of a barge. Once in Krasnoiarsk, Ivan Petrov found his children—his wife had left home in the meantime—and stole their food stamps. What treasure! Then no news.

Five years later, surprise! Ivan Petrov, aka Boris Kouznetsov, is brought back to Norilsk. He had traded his children's foodstamps for authentic-looking forged papers. He had thus become Boris Kouznetsov from Odessa in Ukraine, thousands of miles west from Krasnoiarsk. He was supposed to have left for Khabarovsk in Asia, even thousands of miles further east, by this time. Who could have tracked him there? It was easy for him to find a position as an accountant in some artisan's co-op. In his case, what mattered the most was to go unnoticed. However, complete lack of social contact would have also attracted the attention of the political police. One day as he was sitting at a table, one of the guests told the story of when twenty years earlier, as he was doing his military service, he had narrowly escaped being stabbed by a jealous husband. "It happened to be in your home town," he said, turning to Ivan Petrov, alias Boris Kouznetsov. "I ran off in one of the narrow streets, you know, the one that is just behind the movie theatre *The Radiant Future* on Lenin Avenue, you must know it, don't you?" "Huh," nodded Ivan, embarrassed. Later on, he had been taken aback by some specific questions so that, after the third or fourth time, the ever-present informers had reported his suspicious hesitations. The local police of Khabarovsk had contacted their counterpart in Odessa and soon enough the fake Boris was sentenced to another ten years under the name *Ivan Petrov, aka Boris Kouznetsov.*

All things considered, he was very fortunate. Usually, when taken back to one's former guards, an escaped prisoner is systematically beaten up, sometimes to death, and his corpse is exposed as an example to others at the gates of the compound for several days. Since Boris was arrested thousands of miles away and by other services, he was spared such an unenviable punishment. Given the circumstances, he had fared quite well.

THE SECRET MESSAGE

"And what do you do if one of our soldiers, wounded on the battlefield, refuses your aid and asks you to urgently deliver the secret message he has on him?" Silence. Everyone is too embarrassed to answer. We are in the Fall of 1941, a few months after Nazi Germany invaded Soviet Russia. The administrative center of the forced labor camp of Norilsk is running some training classes for young women, part of the free staff. They will soon be sent to the front as nurses. The person in charge has just taught the protocol for emergency care to be given out to those wounded, heroic defenders of the Motherland (with a capital M). "Well," she resumes, "I will tell you: you leave the wounded and rush to deliver the secret message." "What if he dies?" asks a shy voice. "Exactly. His secret message may contain some information that may save the lives of many red soldiers," the person in charge solemnly claims (1). Now everyone knows what they are supposed to do; the collective takes precedence over the individual. We have known this since kindergarden and we also know that the innumerable secrets coming from the authorities are more important than human lives.

The class was taking place in the large meeting room of the Health Department. Since the heater was out of order, the door of the next room was left open. I happened to be there, painting the walls, a fortuitous chore since I was avoiding working outdoors, digging the frozen Arctic ground for twelve hours straight. I didn't miss a thing that was being said.

Two years later, a new prisoner by the name of Micha is brought to our barracks. He tells us his story: he was on the front, bullets flying around him, subjected to relentless shelling. The security officer had ordered him to carry out a secret message behind the enemy lines. Jovially, he tapped Micha's shoulder and said, "You will be able to forget this hell during your mission. Watch out, though, don't let the enemy kill you or take you! I will be waiting for you with the response." Micha was lucky. He managed to deliver the secret message to its recipient. Oh God, how calm it felt! No sound of bullets flying, as for the shelling it would be heard only in the distance. He wished he could stay a few more days. The sergeant who escorted him to the recipient came back to him and said, "Follow me, soldier!" He took Micha somewhere and locked him in. Surprised, Micha realized he was in a cell. Everything went extremely quickly from that time on. Then, the same old ritual and Micha was accused of being a "defeatist" and received a ten-year sentence in the forced labor camps. How could he possibly suspect that the secret message he had delivered, at the risk of his own life, was a charge against him and, besides, completely fabricated.

Sergei Petrovitch, an old veteran Tchekist who had been swallowed up by the Great Purge of 1937, remembers nostalgically, "We did the same during the Civil War. To avoid seeing armed soldiers take the defence of a comrade we were supposed to arrest, we would entrust him with a secret message reporting him as a counter-revolutionary. I don't recall any of those carriers opening their message and taking off. Some took great risks delivering their message that turned out to be their death sentence..." We were still intrigued by something: if the heroic carrier of the secret message had been wounded and refused help from a trusting heroic nurse ready to fulfill her mission and deliver the message to its recipient, what would have happened to the nurse? Would she have been sentenced to forced labor camps in absentia? For how many years? After all, she was nothing but a substitute.

NOTES
(1) Regarding this subject, it is relevant to note that the Hippocratic oath Soviet doctors take has been somewhat modified. Indeed, following the words "in the interest of the patient," Soviet authorities have added "and society." The interests of society can only be defined by the party and its secret police, so that a doctor who witnesses someone being tortured remains faithful to the Hippocratic oath.

THE LATRINE

The latrine is about a hundred and fifty meters from our barracks. So what, you say. Wait and see.

A sudden urge to urinate wakes Ghulam from his sleep, that deep sleep which is the only thing to make you forget your hunger. Half awake, without getting dressed, he rushes outside and draws some yellow zigzags on the white snow. Unable to control himself he nonetheless strives to reach the latrine when all of a sudden the orderly guards appear and the zigzags stop immediately. They force Ghulam to turn around and take him back to the barracks to get his clothes before they escort him to the cooler for "violation of the rule." He doesn't respond. He knows that the authorities are always right.

It is my turn to rush outside and here I am witnessing Ghulam's procession. The orderlies take me too. I protest. I did nothing and didn't even soil the immaculate whiteness of the snow. They yell, "Shut up!" How dare you claim your innocence! I have been writing to the Communist authorities at all levels for years to protest about my illegal sentence, against the eight years of forced labor camp, then against the official illegal decision at the end of my sentence to keep me "until further notice," and so on.

We are escorted to a cell in the cooler that houses other men, all sentenced for "peeing," whether it is true or not. Gradually we fall asleep and all of a sudden I hear in between snoring, "*Nich'akreb na azrahi kin ast...*" It is Ghulam reciting in a low tone his favorite poet. Both of them were born in Chiraz, Iran, the *zek* Ghulam some seven hundred years after the poet. Ten years ago, he was a pilot in the army of the Shah. Pursued by the Soviet airforce, he was obliged to land in Soviet territory. Ever since, Ghulam has had no news about his family nor has he been able to contact the Iranian consulate. His seclusion in the cooler is difficult as he doesn't know Russian, but only speaks Farsi, French and English. He could pick up some basic Russian in his spare time. I feel he hasn't been destroyed thanks to his incredible will and the surprisingly long list of poems he knows. I am captured by the musical beauty of those Persian stanzas, as majestic as cathedrals, that lift me away from the gore and crude reality of the Gulag and the Soviet state. I manage to translate some of it awkwardly: "The scorpion does not sting someone because he holds a grudge against him but because it's his nature, he cannot be otherwise."

The door to the cell opens. We are now ten prisoners. Ten pairs of arms. That's exactly what the orderly needed to clean the square where the counts are taking place. After an hour the work is finished and they let us go back to our barracks as if nothing had happened.

Waiting for the wake-up signal and another day at work, Wang Pei, a former student at the University Sun-Ya-Sen, recounts that when the Great Wall was being built, the recruiters would visit all the families of peasants around and ask one—only one—of their sons "what noise the chickadee would make if someone twisted its neck, 'tchee or tchoo?'" Whatever the answer, the recruiter would tell him the opposite and the young peasant would leave to build the Great Wall and stay twenty years.

What miracle it is that the reality of the Gulag hasn't managed to erase the distant souvenirs of the Great Wall, nor Saadi's stanza, nor many others... Here probably lies one of the secrets of our survival.

WHAT ABOUT THE OTHER HAND?

"You sweat buckets, and then you take it easy." To avoid forced labor some inmates would cut off their fingers or even a whole hand.

Sergei was a guy people would always listen to and obey without him having to raise his voice. There was nothing special about him and yet, he was surrounded by courtiers ready to serve him. Whenever he felt like a cigarette, immediately someone would roll his cigarette (ready-made ones were rare back then), light it for him and stick it in his mouth, for Sergei had no hands. He was left with two stumps. He never had any protheses—the Gulag had no need for extra hands— so he needed help in the most basic and incongruous situations. For his tobacco supply, most often his courtiers would turn to the pigeons. They would immediately comply without a word. Everyone knew who Sergei was, the most feared of all the thieves in all the compound's barracks. At forty—an age quite seldom reached by a thief—he was most aware of the criminal world and made sure the thieves' laws were strictly observed by all. He remembered numerous cases that set legal precedent so that, indeed, he was an undisputed authority in spite of his physical handicap.

He had an open mind, was interested in all kinds of topics, including things unrelated to the criminal underworld. He enjoyed chatting with the intellectuals who were so numerous among the political prisoners of the Gulag. During one of these conversations, I took the liberty of asking how he had lost his hands. "The left, I cut it off with an axe to avoid doing hard labor. I was a young man back then and it was my first sentence." "What about the other one?" "Because the bastards forced me to carry water with it, I put it under the circular saw…"

THE SURPRISE OF THE PROSECUTOR

1949. I am in the pre-trial prison in the internal prison at one of the district state security administrations of Krasnoiarsk, along the shores of the Yenisei in Siberia. The door to my minuscule cell opens and the officer on duty announces, "The public prosecutor!" He lets in a well-fed man wearing the brown uniform of Soviet justice. "Do you have any questions?" he asks in the standard formal phrase. Well, of course! First of all, I claim my innocence and ask to be freed immediately. The surprised prosecutor reassures me and says, "We are going to verify your claim. If you are innocent, we are going to free up the cell quickly so that we can put someone else in."

I never heard from him again. Months went by. A sheet of ice had formed on the wall of my cell. It got thicker and thicker. Then, a new visit from the public prosecutor. A woman this time. Just like her colleague, she asks me—the same ritual—if I have questions. I complain about the cold, show her the sheet of ice. She looks at it quickly and turns to me, very surprised. "It's obvious it has been raining a lot this past fall and the water has infiltrated the wall, it froze and became ice. What's surprising? You are an educated person and should know about the laws of physics, right?"

TOUFTA: LYING, CHEATING, FORGERY

Here are some anecdotes to illustrate a practice invented by the *zeks* that the Soviet State quickly adopted...

Our camp's administration authorities were competing with the neighbouring ones, something Moscow encouraged. Both had signed written agreements stating that they would strictly follow sanitary regulations and have twelve pest controls a year to fight bedbugs in the barracks. Indeed, millions of bedbugs sucked the blood of the prisoners while they slept. A real plague.

Here's how the sanitary operation took place: the barracks were emptied of their inhabitants. All doors and windows were shut. The openings were taped, and the cells fumigated with sulphur. This corrosive smoke kills the bedbug population in two to three days. Once it's done, all the doors and windows are wide open to let the air in, before the return of the convicts who will, nevertheless, be coughing for a while. What happens to them during the procedure? Well, just like in forced labor camps, empty barracks are scarce during the winter months, so prisoners are placed in smaller groups in already overcrowded cells. In the summer, i.e. in July and August, the Arctic climate allows them to sleep in the open. For some mysterious reason, our camp administration carried out three sanitary operations during the winter months and nine in July and August. A total of twelve, as agreed. The other camp had eleven, at regular intervals. So our camp won.

Here's another story. From 1937 to 1939 I was in Butyrka Prison in Moscow. The authorities would regularly transfer convicts from one cell to another so as to avoid development of mutually supportive groups or any potential regrouping among prisoners. In the midst of those "cell disbandments" I often ran into people who had worked on population censuses, namely the one of 1937 which will ultimately be considered null and void, and, even better, officially forgotten... with good reason since it had counted one hundred and sixty-two millions inhabitants in the USSR whereas in 1934, at the XVIIth Congress of the Communist Party, Comrade Stalin had claimed in person that considering the exceptionally positive economic boom of the country, the Soviet population had reached one hundred and sixty-eight million people. Thousands of members of the Census Commission found themselves sent to the Gulag. Some of them were executed, like the famous Russian statistician O. Krivitkine. In 1939, a new Census Commission then found ten million missing.

Another anecdote goes back quite a long way, into the 1930s, before my arrest. I was in a dacha not far from Moscow with some young devout Communist activists from all over the world, participating in a shooting competition. There were two groups: one with Europeans, another with Chinese. Amongst the Europeans there were some dedicated pacifists who joined the Communist Party precisely because it promised to put an end to all wars. Amongst the Chinese, many had already participated in armed battles and consequently were better shooters than us. Their targets were full of holes, whereas ours were almost completely intact. Our instructor, Captain Ivanov, is very disappointed. He pulls out a big nail from his pocket and makes some holes in our targets before handing them to the jury.

And what about the famous White Sea–Baltic Canal which was completed for operation in 1933 in the twenty-month period Stalin had decreed? This was possible only because OGPU—the State Secret Police of the time—ordered the excavation to be significantly shallower than the original project. The result was that the finished canal was virtually useless (which explains why the Canal was only accessible to shallow barges). Moreover, OGPU made an after-the-fact announcement that the work began – not in 1931, as was the actual case – but in 1932, i.e., OGPU made a sham of the project by presenting false reports.

WHAT A BEAUTIFUL UTOPIA IT WAS!

At the beginning of the 1920s, in Moscow a self-serve market opened just for a couple days. The entrance was free. There were labelled and priced goods displayed, but strangely enough, no cashier at the door. Instead there were glass boxes with a slot for every Soviet citizen—as civic-minded as anyone can be—to put the money in to pay for his articles. At closing time, the revenue exceeded by far the total sales. The same thing happened the next day and the following days, until suddenly it reversed, and revenue declined drastically, causing the shop to close forever.

Why is that? Well, in those remote days, the party was not yet able to gauge the spontaneous enthusiasm of the grassroot activist. The latter believed with his whole heart that from the moment means of production had passed from capitalistic hands to the collective, every citizen had to be noble and honest. Thus, some utopians from the Supply Department in Moscow had tried opening a store without a cashier. Later on, the party of course would put an end to any "spontaneous initiative" which they suspected might provide a means to hide counter-revolutionary plotting at that time (only the Political Bureau could be in charge of organising to perfection any "spontaneous initiative").

Going back to our story... Next to the fanatical utopians, there were also some "realistic" ones. They were the ones who, concerning themselves with the fact that very few citizens had reached the necessary political maturity, they would fill the glass containers with their own rubles so as to avoid the truth coming out, which would in turn provide fuel to the enemy who would claim, "We knew our ideas were nothing but utopian." However, how long can one throw away money in the name of Communist utopia?

Some Communist friends told me about this on my first visit to Moscow in 1929. Like me they would be swallowed by the Great Purge of 1937. Alas, they didn't survive it, but one of the utopians of the former Supply Department of Moscow who strongly believed in the integrity of the citizen freed from capitalism, did survive. I met him in 1955 in a transit prison in Siberia. He hadn't been sentenced for his utopian fantaisies of the 1920s. It wasn't until much later in 1937 that he was sentenced to ten years of prison for "Trotskyism"— very much in fashion at the time—following a fabricated trial. At the end of his sentence, pursuant to an administrative regulation, he was sent to high security prison for another twenty-five years. At sixty he looked like an old man and had lost all his past enthusiasm.

Author's
Drawings

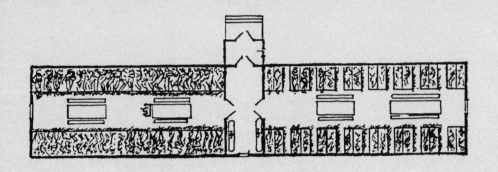

Un zek (prisonnier) par – 45°C.

A **zek** (gulag prisoner) at 45°C below

(Original drawing by Jacques Rossi)

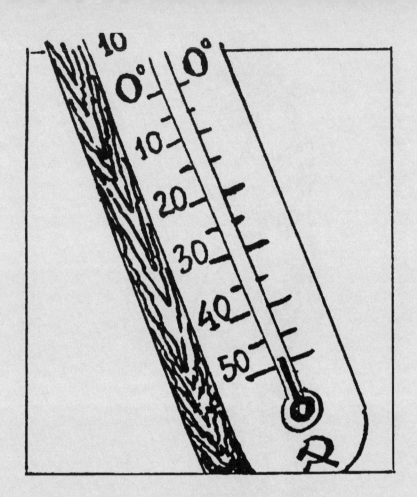

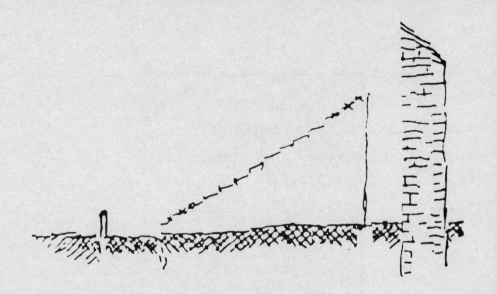

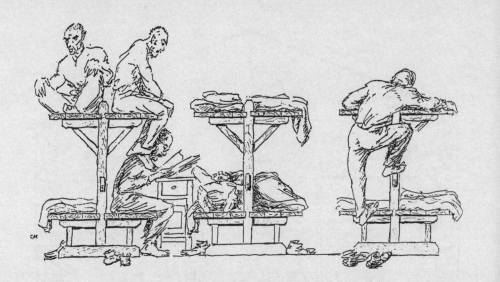

porte fermée

guichet
ouvert

battant-tablette
rabattue

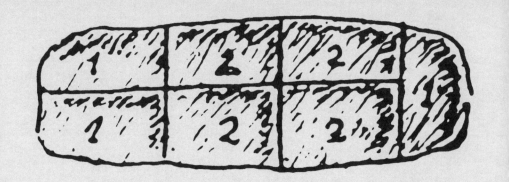

DEAR READER

These *fragments* you have just read are scenes taken from an immense tragedy I witnessed.

I have waited for a rendezvous with the public for a long time. If I survived more than twenty years of intense hardship, it was partly due to my strong will and determination to return to France to tell the tale of what I had seen and learned in the Gulag. *What on earth did I get involved with?* you may ask. Well, my odyssey began in 1937 when, as a young Communist, I became a secret agent for the Comintern (the International Communist Organization). I was ready to sacrifice everything to pursue social justice on earth. If I had been told to jump off the Eiffel Tower to serve the cause, I would have done it without a moment's hesitation. Just like Prometheus, I wanted to steal fire from the gods for mankind's sake and was ready to pay the price for it.

Born in France in 1909 to a well-to-do family, I was ten when the armistice ending the Great War was signed; adults crying "Never again!" left a long-standing impact on me. Later on, I found myself in Warsaw due to family reasons. Back then, social differences in Poland were more blatant than in France, where I would return merely for holidays. One day, on my stepfather's land, an old peasant woman hurried over to kiss my hand. I was barely twelve. At sixteen, I would hang around with young people committed to fighting for social justice. They read Rousseau, the American ethnologist Morgan, and Marx, Engels, Lenin. I remember a sociology student born into a peasant family recounting the misery of the toiling masses. It was a shock to me. I decided to join the then-illegal Polish Communist Party. Six months later I was arrested in Poland for handing out illegal flyers, exhorting young draftees, in case of a war, to turn their weapons not on their brothers – the workers and Soviet peasants – but rather on their real enemies i.e. the capitalists and Polish landowners. I was convicted, sentenced and put in prison for nine months. I was most proud to serve the good cause.

At the end of my sentence, I stopped visiting my stepfather—my mother had died in 1920. In 1928, I was employed in the so-called "technical" department of the Comintern. As such, I travelled around Europe under a number of false identities, carrying documents about which I knew nothing, hidden in inconspicuous objects to be delivered to people I knew nothing about, not even their names. Nor did I try to find out more about them. This was the first rule of revolutionary discipline.

In 1937, in the heat of the Spanish Civil War, I was sent with a secret radio transmitter behind Franco's lines to transmit coded messages to the Republican forces. Then, all of a sudden, I was recalled to Moscow. My traveling companion—whose name I never knew despite the fact that official papers showed us as husband and wife—urged me not to go. It was 1937, the year of the Great Purge. A tidal wave of arrests was inundating the USSR. I was incensed at the "petit-bourgeois" mindset of my comrade. "A soldier of the Revolution always obeys orders, without question!"

Later on in a prison in Moscow, a commissar-interrogator asked me the usual question, "Do you know why you were arrested?" to which I answered no. When I think about it, I wonder if it was because I didn't turn in my companion. "For spying on behalf of France and Poland!" he claimed. I almost burst out laughing. I was sure that soon my comrades would acknowledge their mistake and offer me their apologies. I would tell them that I held no harsh feelings and reassure them that it was inevitable that there be some mistakes considering all the recent happenings, as our valiant comrades strove toward unmasking some tricky plots against the Cause. Some inmates—committed Communists as innocent as I was of the crimes we were accused of—even worried that in this huge mess some true enemies of the people could escape the vigilance of the party. This was even more revolutionary than that "petit-bourgeois" Voltaire, who said that it would be far better to "risk saving a guilty man than to condemn an innocent one."

The party wouldn't acknowledge its "mistake." The error was mine. This I only came to understand gradually, as I discovered what a multitude of people endured because of the Communists by seeing with my own eyes the number of lives crushed because of that regime. During my twenty-four years in the Gulag, I interviewed thousands of fellow inmates—Russians, Ukranians, Tatars, Buryats, just to name a few— from all walks of life—workers, peasants, soldiers, civil servants, party apparatchiks, professors… I heard stories I found hard to believe, thousands of testimonies from all corners of that huge empire which, when pieced together, made a gruesome patchwork of misery.

I slowly became aware that those appealing Communist ideals turned out to be in fact unattainable illusions. Those who insisted on striving to "reach" them would be forced to submit to lying, leading to inevitable censorship and consequently ending in a regime of state terror. Right from its birth, the Soviet Union transformed itself into a huge "Potemkin village," a farcical sham dissimulating oceans of mud and blood. The world's first worker and peasant state, the hope of so many pure souls became the embodiment of a state of absolute deceit. Rather than taking the side of these misled and oppressed people, these "pure souls" preferred to take the side of the Soviet bureaucracy so as to save their sacred illusions.

To think that I had invested all my strength and energy into building a triumphant regime which was just as corrupt and despicable as the Nazis', and even more hypocritical and six times longer, contaminating almost every continent! All things considered, is there any appreciable difference between the millions of victims resulting from these two regimes, whether it be because of the "dirty Nazi traitor collaborator" or the one who, in the Western world, deliberately closed his eyes to support the Soviet regime?

It wasn't until 1985, after my numerous journeys, that I returned to the land of my ancestors to settle down. I discovered, to my great surprise, that the testimony of my experiences interested so few people and was even disturbing to others. "As long as he doesn't fall into the right wing's hands!" some would worry. Others would claim, "It's not right to reveal some questionable facts about the USSR, a country that sacrificed so much to rid Europe of fascism!" Others would interject, persisting in not acknowledging what the critics had suspected for a long time, that if the USSR had helped liberate Europe, it didn't do so out of its own conviction. (1)

I had almost given up hope in getting my story out until the day, in 1995, Jean-Michel Marquebielle came to find me and offered to publish some stories from this volume.

Seventy years ago I committed myself body and soul to the Communist movement, genuinely devoted to defending the cause of social justice. Nothing has changed in that respect. Yet, let's face it: I was led astray and it's now my duty to warn honest people everywhere: "Be careful! Don't get involved on a path that will inevitably lead you to economic, social, political, cultural and ecological catastrophe."

If it hadn't been for all those years spent in the Gulag, I would have had trouble realizing all this.

NOTES

(1) Because France and Great Britain had proposed to Stalin a draft-treaty that set out to thwart the German intentions and to avoid war, he delivered a speech on 19 August 1939 in front of the Politburo, an extract of which follows: "If we sign a pact of mutual assistance with France and Great Britain, Germany will certainly give up on invading Poland and will look for another working agreement with the western powers. The war would then be postponed but, afterwards, events could take a turn for the worse for the USSR.

If we accept, however, the proposal made by Germany and sign a non-agression pact with them, they will obviously attack Poland, inevitably leading to a French and British intervention. Western Europe will thus be the victim of serious troubles and disorders. Under these conditions, we would have a good chance of staying out of the conflict, and could then hope to enter the war at a more advantageous time for us." (Source: *Special USSR Archives*, by T.S. Bouchoueva after the fall of the Soviet regime, see *Novy Mir*, 1994, N° 12, pp. 232-33)

POSTFACE

When Jacques completed his Gulag Handbook, *the result of a most rigorous and colossal work, which he never ceased revising [1], he strived to complete a chore he had in mind for a long time: writing tales staging personal anecdotes from his experience in the Soviet prisons and camps. He then ran into a major difficulty that polyglots may understand: although he spoke French fluently, this was not matched by his writing ability. Being trained as a linguist, he was perfectly aware of this. As a consequence, he sought a "co-author," and, after several inconclusive attempts with various collaborators, once the translation in French of the* Gulag Handbook *was finalized, which was a long haul for us three – Rossi, Véronique Patte and myself–he proposed that I work with him on this new project. It was an experience I shall never forget.*

Surprisingly enough, Jacques could not express his thoughts coherently on paper, nonetheless he knew exactly what result he wanted to achieve. He had a most sensitive knowledge of the French language, though passive in terms of style and syntax.

So we decided to proceed using two complimentary approaches: either he would submit a small piece of text written in approximate French, and we would start from there; or else he would tell me his anecdote, emphasizing some important details, giving me hints as to how to approach the scene, characters, or his own feelings, which I would rewrite to illustrate best his way of thinking and perceiving things while remaining faithful to his original intentions. He would often give me profuse details and further anecdotes which do not appear in the tales here, but that were nonetheless necessary in capturing the right tone. Once each text was written, he would check every sentence scrupulously, expressing approval or giving his criticisms. His disapproval was expressed in a most polite fashion. We could spend hours discussing a passage– not so much the content, but its style. Responsibility for the content was his and his alone. Because his knowledge of the French was most subtle, he knew instinctively when a sentence wasn't right. To get to the heart of the matter was my responsibility, "It's good but it's not exactly that..." he would say without specifying what was wrong. It was up to me to figure it out. I would continue to give him options until he considered one appropriate.

My role in this joint collaboration was strictly formal, I was to set aside my ways of thinking and feeling in order to instead embody his, translating them into words. At times I was not in full agreement, and would have written things differently. In those cases, he would always have the last word, unless his suggestion was grammatically wrong. When dealing with formal respects of the French language, he would always comply with my suggestions.

As a translator, this was a fascinating experience: I had to translate a way of thinking and an understanding of experience into French. If you think about it, this is the essence of my profession— which is to find the right style to convey an approach to, and perception of, the world. Except that this time, I had to do it "live," within the presence of another and his frame of mind, and without the medium of another language. It enabled me to realize the extent to which meaning is reliant upon style— how the choice of a word, adjective or tense of a verb, the presence or absence of a comma, acts on the impression made by a text.

This book, the result of many months of work, could not have been possible without the closeness and respect I felt for Jacques Rossi.

Sophie Benech

NOTES

(1) *Jacques benefited from Perestroika which gave access to the Soviet Archives and the release of new documents, as well as dictionaries of Russian slang forbidden until then. This explains why the French version, which was released later, is slightly different than the original in Russian.*

CHRONOLOGY

10 October 1909: Franciszek Ksawery Heymann was born in Breslau (then German Silesia), third child of Léontine Charlotte Goyet (French, born 1877 in Bourg-en-Bresse), wife of Marcin Heymann, a German-Polish architect.

Early 1920s: Following the independance of the Polish Republic, the Heymann family settles in Warsaw. Death of Léontine Goyet. Heymann is the prefect at Kutno, then director of the Urban Planning Department at the Higher Education Ministry. Franciszek attends the local highschool.

1927: Applies to the Academy of Fine Arts in Poznan. Joins the undercover Polish Communist Party after a stint with the TUR [Workers' Universities Union] and the Polish Socialist Party. Arrested for handling out pamphlets calling for young recruits to get involved and secede.

20-21 October 1928: Trial. Sentenced to nine months of prison. Released after six months.

1929: Studies at the Krakow School of Fine Arts; sent to Berlin by the Communist Party.

1930-1936: Recruited by the Comintern who "lends" him to the secret services of the Red Army; he travels throughout Europe performing "technical missions" while pursuing his studies in several European universities, among them the Berlin Fine Arts Academy, the Paris Academy of Oriental Languages (Ecole des Langues Orientales) receiving a diploma under an assumed name, Cambridge University in England (1932), and the Academy of Oriental Languages in Moscow.

13 April 1937: Liaison Agent with the Spanish Republicans in Valladolid.

14 November 1937: Summoned to Moscow.

From December 1937 to April 1939: Arrested in Moscow under the identity of Jacques Robertovitch Rossi, imprisoned at the Lubyanka, then at the Butyrka, and sentenced by the OSSO (OGPU Special Board) to eight years of hard labor camp according to Article 58, line 6, that is to say, accused of spying for the French and Polish governments.

7 April 1939: Departure via a Stolypin freight car to an unknown destination that turns out to be the Arctic zone, passing through many transit prisons: Kirov, Sverdlosk, Novossibirsk, Omsk, Krasnoyarsk. Arrival at the transit camp of Krasnoyarsk on the Yenisei river. Convoy to the port of Doudinka, part of the Norilsk camp, 70th north parallel.

1939 to 1947: Confinement to the Norilsk camp. His sentence officially ends in 1945, but is extended through a special decree "until further notice." Conditional release 15 April 1947, coupled with the suspension to leave Norilsk.

1947 to 1949: He works in Norilsk (from 25 August 1947 to 22 June 1948 as an official translator specialized in engineering; from 22 June 1948 to 29 September 1948 as geotechnician; and from 29 September 1948 to 20 March 1949 as photographer).

1949 to 1956: New arrest. Confinement in the pretrial prison of Norilsk where he goes on his first hunger strike in 1949 to obtain the official statement of his verdict. Transfer to Krasnoyarsk Prison. New sentence of 25 years in the Gulag for "spying for the French, the English and the Americans." Brief stay in the Irkoutsk Prison, then transfer to the Aleksandrovka Central. After Stalin's death in 1953, second hunger strike to obtain his liberation. In 1955, transport to Moscow via various transit prisons (Irkoutsk, Krasnoyarsk, Novossibirsk, Smirnov, Ekaterinenbourg, Kirov, etc.), Central Penitentiary of Vladimir.

1959–1961: Under house arrest, he is sent to Samarkand where he files to be repatriated to Poland. Third hunger strike. Sends a telegram to Krouchtchev asking for an exit visa.
February 1961: Repatriated to Communist Poland.

1st September 1964–30 September 1977: Professor of French Literature at the University of Warsaw. Joins the Polish Communist Party. Back in France for a workshop in Grenoble followed by several short visits to France. Starts writing in Russian the future *Gulag Handbook*, originally conceived as a dictionary of slang.

30 September 1977: Leaves Poland.

1978: Stays in Japan with his best friend, Misao Gosuke Uchimura, a former Japanese war prisoner he met in the Gulag.

1979–1985: Stays in the USA, New York and Washington D.C. Hosted by Georgetown University, he completes his *Gulag Handbook*.

25 May 1985: Comes back definitively to France with a residential visa, in the Drôme then Marseille.

1987: *Spravotchnik po Gulagu [The Gulag Handbook]* is published in Russian in London (Overseas Publications). He lives in Paris rue Edgar Poe, in the 19th arrondissement.

November 1988: Moves to 22 Avenue de la Résistance, in Montreuil (outside of Paris) until 2001.

9 August 1990: Regains his French nationality.

1993: *Spravotchnik po Gulagu [The Gulag Handbook]* is released in Russia.

1995: Publishes *Fragments de vies, vingt ans dans les camps soviétiques* (Elikia Publishers, Paris, France).

1996: *The Gulag Handbook* is released in Japanese (Keigado Publishers, Tokyo, Japan).

1997: *Le Manuel du Goulag [The Gulag Handbook]* is translated into French and published in France (Cherche midi éditeur).

2000: A second augmented edition of *Fragments de vies, vingt ans dans les camps soviétiques* with twenty two new texts is renamed *Qu'elle était belle, cette utopie!* (Cherche midi éditeur).

21 June 2001: Suffers a stroke that leaves him diminished physically but not mentally. Moves to St Casimir in Paris, an elderly home run by Polish nuns.

March 2002: Publishes with Michèle Sarde *Jacques le Français, pour mémoire du Goulag* (Cherche midi éditeur).

2003: The augmented edition of *Qu'elle était belle cette utopie! is published in Italian as Com'era bella questa utopia!* (Marsilio Editori, Venice, Italy)

30 June 2004: Jacques Rossi dies in Paris.
2004: *Qu'elle était belle cette utopie!* is translated into Japanese and published by Keigado Publishers (Tokyo, Japan).

SOON TO BE PUBLISHED

Matěj Spurný: Making the Most of Tomorrow. A Laboratory of Socialist
Modernity in Czechoslovakia
Petr Roubal: Spartakiads. The Politics of Physical Culture in Communist
Czechoslovakia
Olivier Mongin: The Urban Situation
Miroslav Petříček: Philosophy en noir
Martin C. Putna: Rus - Ukraine - Russia. Scenes from the Cultural History
of Russian Religiosity